Pot–shots at the Preacher

Pot-shots at the Preacher

James Allen Sparks

Abingdon / Nashville

POTSHOTS AT THE PREACHER

Copyright © 1977 by Abingdon

All rights reserved.
No part of this book may be reproduced in any manner whatsoever without written permission of the publisher except brief quotations embodied in critical articles or reviews. For information address Abingdon, Nashville, Tennessee.

Library of Congress Cataloging in Publication Data

Sparks, James A 1933–
   Potshots at the preacher.

   Bibliography: p.
   1. Pastoral theology. 2. Clergy—Psychology. 3. Church controversies.
I. Title.
BV4011.S6   253'.2   76-30753

ISBN 0-687-33240-0

The chart on page 98 was devised by G. H. Woodard and originally appeared in *Action Information*. Used by permission of the Alban Institute.

Scripture quotations unless otherwise noted are from the Revised Standard Version Common Bible, copyrighted ©1973.

Scripture quotations noted TEV are from Today's English Version of the New Testament. Copyright © American Bible Society 1966, 1971.

MANUFACTURED BY THE PARTHENON PRESS AT
NASHVILLE, TENNESSEE, UNITED STATES OF AMERICA

To Pauline and Beth
. . . Loving Critics

Contents

Preface *9*

PART ONE: Coping with Criticism

1. Introduction *13*
2. How We Perceive Criticism *16*
3. The Futility of Avoiding Criticism *31*
4. Trusting Your Feelings *35*
5. Why Criticism Comes *53*
6. The Super-Negative Critic *65*
7. Criticism and the Minister's Wife *75*

PART TWO: Letting Criticism Work for You

8. Can Criticism Help? *88*
9. Growing the Minister–Parish Relationship *97*
10. Closing the Perfection Gap *110*
11. When You Feel Critical *116*
    Notes *119*
    Resources *123*
    Bibliography *126*

Preface

This book is about one facet of human experience many find troublesome—coping with criticism. Written from the minister's perspective—ministers frequently attract criticism—it discusses how we are likely to respond to it, why we are so sensitive to it, and how we can use it to grow as persons.

Coping with criticism is not the same as coping with conflict. People can disapprove, be disappointed, or become frustrated without being in conflict. Yet criticism is difficult to manage because it carries the implication of personal failure. And in spite of its promise of hope, acceptance, and forgiveness, the church doesn't really handle criticism or conflict very well.

Whether you are a minister or minister's spouse (I use the term "minister" in this book generically to designate all who serve in religious vocations, *i.e.,* lay leader, priest, rabbi, or member of a religious order), coping with criticism is part of your life. And it can hurt!

In a recent survey of over one hundred clergy, spouses, and members of religious orders participating in a University of Wisconsin-Extension Educational Telephone Network program on intimacy, 81 percent said they occasionally experienced hostile, blaming criticism.

Twenty-five percent affirmed that this was the single most difficult personal problem they had to manage. More than 35 percent said that coping with their feelings of inadequacy was a central personal issue. This sample is probably representative; few of us are exempt.

In the first section I discuss the hurtful aspects of criticism and its impact on the person being criticized. With some detail I explore the temporary emotional disorganization that often results from critical confrontation. Likewise, I discuss some of the factors that can cause persons to be irrationally negative in giving criticism.

Although Part I concentrates more on coping with hostile, blaming criticism that is frequently undeserved, Part II looks at the helpfulness of negative confrontation and its impact upon personal growth as well as growth of the minister–congregation relationship.

The ideas presented in this book will undoubtedly stimulate parish leaders to discuss with their boards and committees how their groups handle negative feelings. Is there a willingness and an openness to confront the emotional issues that arise in relationships? Or is it peace at any price?

Some churches, taking one unhealthy approach, avoid confronting the minister until feelings erupt precipitously; then they think the only way to manage criticism is to take potshots from a distance or to fire the minister and start over again. Based on the premise that people and organizations cannot please everyone, another approach advocates that clergy and laity mutually confront one another by exploring expectations and giving feedback. Even when it is negative, direct expression of feedback is essential if relationships in the church are to have vitality and integrity and persons are to be affirmed within the community of believers.

Though this book is written for clergy and church leaders, members of other helping professions, such as social workers, health care persons, public school teachers, and rural mental-health workers, may find striking similarities between

PREFACE

clergy and themselves in coping with criticism. By writing for the profession of which I'm a member and exposing my own frailties, I have tried to speak to a common human experience. I hope you will find it useful.

Candid criticism of many friends and colleagues has made this book possible. In addition, I gratefully acknowledge the contribution of Eleanor Vogt, University of Wisconsin-Extension Health and Social Services Agent; Lloyd Rediger, Office of Pastoral Services, Wisconsin Council of Churches; Jerold Apps, Professor of Adult Education, University of Wisconsin; Speed Leas, Institute of Advanced Pastoral Studies; and Mark Rouch, Interpreter's House.

I am also grateful to university associates Victor Howery and Roger Williams who have had no small part in my personal growth and to William Blockstein who supported each step of the way.

J.A.S.
University of Wisconsin-Extension
Madison, Wisconsin

PART ONE
Coping with Criticism

Chapter 1
Introduction

I have personally experienced criticism and observed its effect on fellow ministers in fifteen years of parish ministry. As a young pastor with a seminary degree in hand and a call from a small rural church, I engaged in a private conspiracy to avoid criticism. The problem was that neither I nor those I invited to conspire with me were aware of my need to avoid it.

Experiences in the ministry I thought were unique only to me are shared in various guises by clergy and their spouses. As a continuing-education specialist at the University of Wisconsin-Extension, I have met with clergy groups statewide. The fear of criticism and the reality of its emotional impact surfaces again and again. Nevertheless, clergy and spouses seem more willing today to speak openly of the problems and dilemmas they face, less inclined to play a role. I met recently with a group of small-town clergy wives who wanted to form a support group. I was amazed at how quickly the group moved to a level of intimacy where several spoke of how they were or had been in psychotherapy. The women did not force disclosure, but encouraged one another with their acceptance.

Since many clergy have no one who is pastor to them

POTSHOTS AT THE PREACHER

(research shows that married ministers most often turn to their spouses), this book is intended to be a companion and guide to those feeling the stress of critical confrontation. Most of us can handle some criticism—depending on what it is and who is giving it. None of us can avoid negative messages entirely. But some messages are more negative than others and may be undeserved. This kind of criticism hurts! In finding new ways of receiving, accepting, or rejecting criticism, you may learn about yourself and how you react under this particular kind of stress. If we can better understand our own motivations, our assumptions about human relationships, and what caring in ministry means, then we can more fully love, live, and grow when criticism comes. And come it will!

Last summer my wife, daughter, and I took the Crystal River canoe trip at Waupaca, Wisconsin. We boarded a canopied launch for the half-hour ride through the Chain-of-Lakes to the river mouth, the fifteen small fiberglass canoes bobbing behind like peapods in a bathtub. I was apprehensive since none of us is a canoeist, but the brochure promised "fun for the whole family." Not being a swimmer, I asked the usual questions about the depth of the river, life jackets, and the severity of the rapids. What "fun for the whole family" meant became uncomfortably clear as our launch neared the river.

Where was the pier? There wasn't one! The launch slowly approached ripples marking the river's entrance and gently anchored its bow into the sandy bottom. Picking up the intercom speaker, the captain announced: "Some people think they can make this trip without getting wet. If you're one of them, you'd better go back with me." No one did; we were committed.

The trip was an eleven-mile fumble as we hit boulders, turned over, and tried again. Shooting the first rapids was a psychological triumph. Hearing their roar just ahead, I wanted

INTRODUCTION

to go to shore, but something compelled me to go on. The little canoe jerked against a rock, turned around, and pitched stern first into the whirlpool at the end. There we swamped, slowly sinking to the sandy bottom, our heads barely above the water, each accusing the other of gross navigation error. Then we laughed and, after much effort, righted our canoe and went on. The captain was right; it's impossible to take the Crystal River trip without getting wet.

Going through life as a minister or minister's spouse without evoking some form of disapproval is like going down the Crystal River without getting wet. It can't be done! As normal, healthy human beings, we care how others feel about us. In a religious career or being related to it by marriage, we tend to be acutely sensitive about the impressions we make and the feelings we incite in others. When these impressions and feelings come as faultfinding and blaming, then what is said, how it is communicated, and to whom becomes terribly important.

Chapter 2
How We Perceive Criticism

When criticism comes, we are likely to perceive it in two ways—either as a helpful response to an error or mistake that we have made or as an unjust evaluation of us. How we perceive criticism largely determines how we will handle it. If we accept another's negative message as a legitimate response to a mistake, then we can integrate this into our experience and go on with something else. But if we feel we have been put upon or put down unfairly, then we are likely to experience stress.

Distaste for criticism is closely tied to the need for approval, respect, and esteem from others. All of us have a need to be liked, to seek the approval of those at home and at work. We want affirmation that we are competent and good at what we do. When we get messages that we are not measuring up, that we haven't fulfilled expectations, we experience what Reuel Howe calls "diminishment of being." It's the feeling of once again being a bad little girl or boy.

Nearly forty years ago, Karen Horney identified the "fear of disapproval" as a common theme in neuroses. The fear of disapproval is a neurotic and compulsive attempt to manipulate self and others to avoid criticism, which is expressed in the need to be right. Horney says, "Usually a person of this type is

HOW WE PERCEIVE CRITICISM

unable to endure the slightest differences of opinion, or even a difference of emotional emphasis, because in his thinking even a minute disagreement is equivalent to a criticism."[1]

As I reflect on my own early motivations for entering the ministry, I discover that my need for approval—or fear of disapproval—may have significantly influenced my pursuing a church vocation.

Public speaking in church as a youth brought praise from the minister, older members of the church, and friends. The church provided a prepackaged community of warmth and security. I never really considered the possibility there was another world out there—a world in which religious, good-intentioned people could at times be ill-tempered, disapproving, even spiteful.

Seminary in the mid-fifties didn't do much to dispel this idealized fantasy. As a first-year student, I worked part time in a newly organized church just outside Pittsburgh. Since only travel and expenses, but no salary, was paid, everything my wife and I did was appreciated.

The pastor appreciated the extra staff assistance, and the board appreciated the additional calling in the communtiy; we couldn't do much wrong. In the remaining two years of seminary, I had little opportunity to experience negative feedback from persons receiving my services. Seminary had taught me how to evaluate biblical and theological thought, but not how to handle the disapproval of people who felt I was neglecting them or in other ways letting them down.

Related to Needs

Criticism is any message intended to express a disapproving evaluation. The one giving the criticism may intend to be helpful or may wish to hurt and punish. One may disapprove of something we have said or done as well as what we didn't say or do. Criticism can come in broad, general strokes, such as "You never smile when you greet people at the door," or in more specific messages, such as "You didn't smile at me last Sunday."

A negative message is usually directed toward some failing or weakness. According to psychologist Everett Shostrom, criticism can be given with or without feeling. He says the absence of feeling in criticism is evident by its needling or bitchy quality; it rarely communicates the sender's real feelings.[2] Or does it?

It is important to keep in mind that personal criticism usually comes to us because we have disappointed someone, or we have deviated from the usual, the expected, the traditional. When criticism comes it carries a specific statement of another's intention toward us. If not specifically stated, the intention may be veiled. For example, when someone says, "You never smile when you greet people at the door," that person may mean, "You never smile when I greet you; I'd like for you to smile at me!" or, "I would like for you to pay more attention to me."

Our reaction to criticism—even as mild as this—is influenced by our attitude toward ourselves and life in general. I like the term "life agenda" as a way of talking about how we respond to life in a given time-frame. For example, during the past few weeks I may have been feeling down, unsure of myself, even panicky about self-diagnosed inadequacies. Or I may be worried about the health of a family member or about accumulating debts. These "worries" or needs can prevent us from thinking beyond how we are going to get through the day. Any additional stress becomes a further assault on our ability to cope with the moment. The person who may be at what Abraham Maslow calls the coping-survival level of living

HOW WE PERCEIVE CRITICISM

will have a difficult time with criticism, regardless of how innocuous it might be.

According to Maslow, coping-survival needs are those that promote physical well-being, such as food, shelter, sex, sleep, and oxygen. The person who is struggling to meet these needs has little inclination or energy to satisfy other hungers. It is difficult to read a book or write poetry when you are hungry and dreaming of food. Safety needs are next in the hierarchy. These are expressed by the need to live in a fairly consistent world with a certain amount of routine.

When physiological and safety needs are met, then the higher, growth-producing needs emerge. Relationships with people are important; Maslow agrees with Carl Rogers that to be loved is "being deeply understood and deeply accepted." Love in a relationship is a giving of self to the other in trust and the absence of defenses. It is taking the risk of being vulnerable by dropping masks and pretenses.

Next in the hierarchy of needs common to each of us are self-respect and esteem from other people. We need to feel that we are good at what we do, that we are competent, achieving, and have some mastery of skills or knowledge. On the other hand, we want others to appreciate us and reinforce our good feelings about ourselves. Maslow believes that the most healthy self-esteem comes from respect that has been earned and is therefore deserved.

Self-actualization is a trigger word that Maslow uses to conceptualize psychological growth, development, and utilization of potential powers. He uses many words to describe people who live at this higher plane—wholeness, perfection, completion, justice, aliveness, richness, simplicity, playfulness, self-sufficiency, uniqueness, and beauty. Self-actualizing people are no longer just coping with their world; they're having fun in life.[3]

POTSHOTS AT THE PREACHER

Factors That Influence Perception of Criticism

Most of us live out our lives somewhere between two extremes on a life-agenda continuum. At any given time we are somewhere between coping-survival—struggling with basic physical and safety needs—and being self-fulfilled, which motivates us to expand our vision and to welcome change and growth.

It is not always easy to identify your life-agenda except through vague inner signals. If you are feeling nervous, insecure, depressed, and generally disconsolate about life and if most of your thought-energy is on just getting through the day, you're probably solidly into the coping-survival agenda. If, on the other hand, you are enjoying the present and look forward to tomorrow and if you sense inner strength, then you're probably well into the self-fulfillment agenda.

Some current research suggests that we move back and forth between these two points according to natural rhythms in our lives. We cannot sustain peak experiences; occasionally we have to experience the valleys of life. Both the peaks and the lows can move us toward change and growth.

Criticism that is directed towards us, or is perceived as such, is one external force that can cause movement in our life-agenda by provoking stress (see fig. 1). There are at least six factors or filters, however, through which we perceive criticism. They are—

1. feelings about yourself;
2. sensitivity to inadequacies;
3. blurring the targets of criticism;
4. past responses;
5. context in which criticism is given;
6. assessing the power of others.

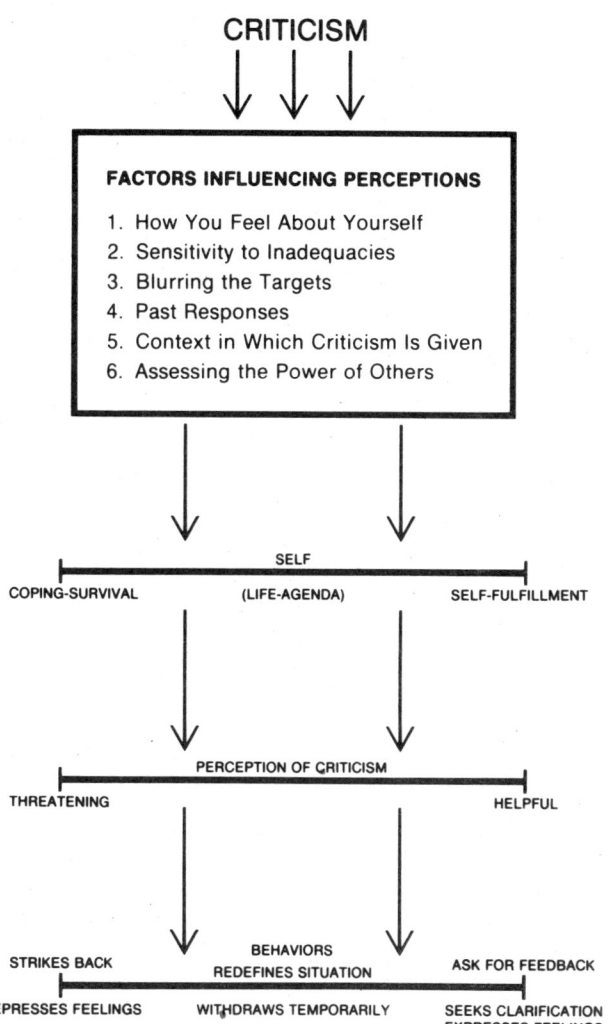

Fig. 1. **How We Perceive Criticism**

POTSHOTS AT THE PREACHER

Filtered through any one or combination of these six factors, criticism is then perceived to be somewhere on a continuum between "threatening" and "helpful." If the negative message "I think you're driving too fast for this road" is given to one hundred drivers, it is possible there would be as many perceptions of that criticism as those who heard it. The resulting behavior would reflect how it was perceived and accepted. Some would view it as an unfair attack on their driving while others would see it as helpful.

How You Feel About Yourself

How you feel about yourself at the moment you receive criticism is crucial to how you are likely to accept it. Do you feel relaxed and together or tense and nervous? Do you feel confident and expansive or uneasy and withdrawn? If your attitudes and moods are out of tune, even the mildest form of feedback may be distorted and taken as crisis-provoking criticism, even if you consider yourself to be generally calm.

Knowing yourself is being in tune with your feelings even when such feelings seem to be incongruent with being a minister. For example, you may experience an angry feeling toward a parishioner, but your concept of ministry may push you to deny this anger. Knowing yourself is the beginning to accepting your weaknesses and rejoicing in your strengths. It makes you feel stronger.

Another example of knowing yourself is being aware of how you react in certain situations and with different people. It is being aware of your own chemistry and your reactions when mixed with the chemistry of others. I am a "delayed reaction" person. I don't feel the impact of criticism until two or three days later. Then it really hits me. Knowing this, I have learned to expect to feel uncomfortable and prepare for it.

HOW WE PERCEIVE CRITICISM

Sensitivity to Inadequacies

Another factor that influences how we take criticism is how sensitive we are to our own inadequacies. When my wife disapproves of how I select my tie for the day, I don't view this behavior as threatening to my self-image. I may be amused or slightly annoyed; I can integrate it into the moment. If I feel inadequate about clothes or inadequate in some other area, however, then I may get peeved.

Donald Smith's *Clergy in the Crossfire* has summarized an impressive amount of research that presents today's minister as a person who is burdened by feelings of inadequacy. It is an inadequacy borne out of role conflicts. The role of minister carries with it a tradition of expectations. Society expects that its ministers, priests, and rabbis will be competent preachers, liturgists, counselors, and teachers and that they will effectively relate to people of all ages. Feelings of inadequacy arise when the individual experiences conflict between the person he understands himself to be and the role he feels required to play.[4]

According to Smith, much of the research in the last ten years has differentiated among the dimensions of this role conflict, such as (1) the importance laity and clergy attach to each of the roles, including ideal concepts of ministry, (2) the amount of time spent in various roles, (3) the role most enjoyed, (4) the relationship of personal expectations to those of laity, and (5) the satisfaction in measuring up to his own expectations.

An early report of the Northeast Career Center at Princeton, one of the first clergy career-counseling centers, identified the fear of failure among the crises experienced by over one thousand clients. Many of us live in dread that criticism will come in those areas of our work where we most fear failure.

POTSHOTS AT THE PREACHER

Any negative message calling attention to a sensitive area may be readily perceived as a judgment of failure, a prophecy of fear come true. The response isn't "How can I use this criticism to be a better preacher or counselor or administrator?" but "How can I survive knowing that others affirm the inadequacy I feel about myself?" This fear is substantiated by psychologist Sidney Jourard who says that if others know us as we know ourselves, we risk being "divorced, fired, inprisoned, or shot."[5] Criticism that strips us naked, revealing our blemishes, becomes crisis-provoking, and our response is more survival-oriented than growth-directed.

All the years I was a parish pastor I lived in suspended dread that my nervousness in visiting the sick, my intense unease around hospitals, would be found out. I faithfully made rounds, but I confess it was more to relieve my own anxiety than to comfort the patient. The people I called on seemed conforted and their needs of the moment at least partially met. Nevertheless, the uneasy feeling never really went away, nor did my foreboding that some day others might discover my inadequacy.

In my role as hospital caller, even the slightest suggestion that I had fallen short of expectations would have been crisis-provoking. On the other hand, had I felt secure in this traditional and revered function of ministry, I might have accepted a reasonable evaluation of my bedside manner as an opportunity for improvement and therefore changed my behavior.

Blurring the Targets of Criticism

How do you know who or what is the real target of another's criticism? How do you know if the critic is judging your actions, attacking you personally, complaining about the church program, or displacing personal anger onto you? For

HOW WE PERCEIVE CRITICISM

clergy and spouses, such blurring is common. The functions of ministry have become so much a part of the person that it is difficult to separate self from work roles so that any criticism of behavior in a role becomes blurred into an assault on self. Some of the studies at the University of Chicago in the fifties by Eugene Friedmann and Robert Havighurst indicate that the higher one is in the occupational hierarchy, the more one's sense of identity is merged with occupation. Work is a way of life.

Bob and Linda, whom I met for the first time about two years ago at a continuing-education planning meeting, illustrate the grim consequences of sacrificing self to the roles and functions of parish ministry. An attractive couple in their early thirties, they were noticeably silent during the first half hour of the meeting called to plan for a one-day program on the problems and pressures of ministers' families. Everyone else was freely sharing how they experienced pressure and discomfort.

Finally, Linda interjected: "Being a minister's wife is my whole life. I've never experienced any criticism or unhappiness as long as we've been at this church." As she spoke, she used such phrases as "our ministry," "my women's group," and "our high calling." She viewed her heavy involvement in the church as God's call to spiritual service. Unequivocally, she said, "Our work is my life."

Several months later I was surprised to discover that Bob and Linda had enrolled in a two-day marriage communication workshop I was co-leading. They seemed a withdrawn couple, but listened attentively to the presentations and with encouragement participated in the brief practice sessions. About midway through the second day, they were asked to talk for a few minutes before the group on some old or new issue between them as means of practicing effective communication skills. The conversation lasted only ten minutes, but all of us knew that Bob and Linda were in the midst of a real crisis. We learned that they had recently moved to a new church. Instead of acceptance and appreciation, which they chronicled eight months earlier, they now felt resistance and hostility. Linda, especially, had discovered that her desire to lead and be involved was not shared by the church women. Bob was doubting his competence to lead the congregation and considered leaving the ministry. Even in this brief, limited exchange, Linda's voice betrayed her grief. For Bob to give up being a pastor meant she had to give up the one thing in life that defined her identity—the role of minister's wife.

They interpreted criticism as an assault on their worth as people. So inextricably were their self-images tied to the roles of minister and clergy spouse, any evaluation of how those roles were performed threatened their being.

Past Responses to Criticism

How you responded to past criticism may affect your present attitudes toward it. As a child, how did you react when your parents or teachers disapproved of your behavior? Psychiatrist-writer Allen Wheelis describes his residual feelings long after his father's death:

My father and I have never parted. He made his mark on me that summer, and after his death that fall continued to speak on a high-fidelity system within my conscience, speaks to me still, tells me that I have been summoned, that I am standing once again before him on that glass porch giving an account of myself, that I will be found wanting, still after all these years a "low-down, no-account scoundrel," and that this judgment will be binding on my view, that I shall not now or ever be permitted to regard myself as innocent or worthy.[6]

HOW WE PERCEIVE CRITICISM

My first exposure to criticism by a teacher came in the first grade. It had been raining, and she warned us to stay away from the big mudhole during recess. Two or three of us thought we'd at least go look at it. I was standing at the edge when one of the bigger boys ran by and pushed me in. I felt guilty and humiliated as I faced the teacher who sternly reprimanded me for my disobedience. I tried to explain, but the words choked in my throat. I knew I wasn't to blame, but would she or my parents believe me?

As I reflect on early schooling experiences, I find a pattern of behavior directed toward pleasing and earning approval. If there were extra work to be done, I did it; if speech or writing contests were offered, I entered them.

Nine years separated the second humiliating experience from the first. It was the third week of ninth-grade algebra class. I had graduated from a small neighborhood school to a very large senior-high school. Life was fast-paced in a strange new environment. Going to the rest room required a hall pass. The building was big, the principal awesome, and I felt vulnerable. One afternoon, the teacher called me to the blackboard. I didn't want to go; I didn't understand the problem. But he said **"GO,"** and I went. After I managed several unsuccessful attempts at the problem, he came up to me, face flushed, and pounded his fist on the board. "You goose, can't you get that problem straight?" he demanded. I tried to offer an explanation, but dissolved in tears right in front of my friends and everyone.

I never cried again in school. But I have continued to be overly sensitive to the approval of people in authority—teachers, parish board members, community leaders. Sometimes I still catch myself in some approval-seeking behavior asking inwardly, "Why am I taking this to the teacher?"

POTSHOTS AT THE PREACHER

Context in Which Criticism Is Given

The situational context—physical setting, timing, and support processes—out of which criticism comes is important in whether we perceive it as helpful or diminishing. Unfortunately, we cannot always choose the time or place for expressions of disapproval or anger in others. It may come when we are least expecting it, catching us off guard, trapped in our own embarrassment and feeling helpless, especially if others witness the encounter. Negative messages at best are difficult to receive in private, but when they come as a surprise in public they are difficult to manage.

I first experienced this feeling of helplessness soon after I began work in my first parish. For several months, our small semirural church had planned an ushering program that organized all the men and teen-age boys in teams, each taking turns at the weekly worship service. We elected to initiate the plan at the next Communion service. As I greeted parishioners at the door following that service, I felt good.

My emotional high, however, was short-lived. One member of the board, a person who worked unselfishly with the youth, was last to speak with me. Eyes so angry they were filled with tears, face reddened, and voice shaking he announced loudly that the morning was a fiasco. The ushers had performed incompetently, and the service had lost its "spiritual" quality. Besides, he continued, what right did I as a new minister have to upset other people with my ideas? Then he unloaded a list of personal grievances.

As he spoke, I could feel the authority and power I had experienced during the service slowly drain from me. My knees felt rubbery, and my breath choked in my throat. How could I respond? I learned later that he had been ushered to the wrong pew, one seat removed from where he and his family sat for more than forty years. His displaced anger had focused on

HOW WE PERCEIVE CRITICISM

me rather than on the real reason—the disruption of a forty-year routine. I felt hurt and betrayed by a man I considered a friend, a man who used a public occasion to unload feelings, leaving me little room to move. I confess I was also trapped by a self-expectation that a minister should be cool and controlled in such situations. Instead, I felt weak and sick.

Assessing the Power of Others

Another factor affecting how we accept criticism is one of which we may not be aware. It is how we perceive the power of others. Settling into a new work situation, we meet many people for the first time in a variety of settings—receptions, social events, worship services, committee meetings. We form first impressions, among them whether this person or that is perceived as a potential risk to our inner sense of security and well-being or as a person who will be helpful.

Many ministers face the dilemma of not knowing who is the boss, the one person to be accountable to. In the absence of such a person within the structure of the local church or parish, they are likely to turn for approval to people who occupy positions of authority in the church and community. Some denominations have tried to meet this void by providing for pastoral-relations committees to be a point of reference for the minister. These committees act as a go-between to mediate conflicts between parish and pastor and be a friend to the minister.

Where such committees do not exist another phenomenon takes over. Almost unconsciously, we strive to develop relationships among people who have power, who are recognized by the church and the community as leaders. We identify those with whom we feel comfortable and who seem comfortable with us; we are also aware of those whose relationship with us is distant and guarded. We tend to respond

POTSHOTS AT THE PREACHER

in like manner, more out of our clergy role than anything else. When our inner antennae signal "risk," we are likely to react in ways to avoid the other person's threatening or aggressive behavior.

For example, we may visit that person more frequently than other members of the church in hopes of eliminating this pastoral function from possible criticism, especially if we don't number regular home visits among our priorities. For another, we might act deferentially toward that person with blandishments of praise and ingratiating sentiments.

Being aware of our inner signals, especially when we're under fire, is difficult. It is clear, however, that criticism interjects significant stress into our lives and sometimes causes us to engage in coping-survival activity. Such activity diverts our concentration in work and personal life and siphons valuable creative energy that could be applied to other tasks. In the following chapters we will examine some common coping mechanisms and suggest alternatives for managing destructive as well as helpful criticism.

Chapter 3
The Futility of Avoiding Criticism

No one likes pain, physical or mental. If we have a headache or muscle spasm, we may try to relieve it with an aspirin. If we feel unusually shaky or nervous, we may take a mild tranquilizer or divert our attention by going for a drive or shopping for something extravagant. Pain is how nature warns us of stress on our physical or mental system. Medications and diversions may temporarily relieve symptoms, but the causes of the stress remain.

Thinking we can avoid criticism is closely akin to what Nena and George O'Neill call the "maturity myth." According to these authors, the maturity myth is an illusion based on a static rather than a dynamic attitude to life. It promises that at some point in our lives we will arrive at a plateau that is identified by these characteristics: (1) We'll be home safe by the time we're in our forties, (2) We'll be less restless and more stable, (3) We'll have emotional security, (4) Our sex life will be safe, and (5) Our future will be manageable. According to the myth, the optimum age for this state of tranquility is around forty, depending on where one is in relation to that magical number.[1]

Variations of this notion take the form of what I call "avoidance myths" for the minister and spouse. This is the hope that at some time and some place stress-inducing criticism won't have to be experienced. Key elements in this myth are as follows:

1. The harder you work, the greater the rewards.
2. Criticism means failure.
3. Things will be different in a new church.
4. Criticism must be avoided.

Myth: Hard Work Is Rewarded

Some people try to stave off criticism by hard work and long hours. Wayne Oates used the designation "workaholic" to describe the person whose inner motivations drive him or her to excessive work activity.[2] Such compulsion is two-edged—to stay the inevitable by taking away one possible cause and, if failing to do that, to reduce any pangs of guilt resulting from it.

I have known ministers who, under severe pressure to produce, to be nice, or to counter criticism, have written long "pastoral letters" reciting how hard they've labored in the Lord's service and have concluded their appeal with an invitation to reconciliation. The problem with work addiction is that it rarely achieves its goals. We may put in the hours, but our productivity rarely reflects the investment of time and energy.

Myth: Criticism Means Failure

The ministry is one occupation in which the system of evaluation and rewards is very confused. Although many denominations provide for an annual review of the minister's work, this is often performed hastily by a small committee without much preparation and with great embarrassment. Salary adjustments tend to be small, based on "what the

THE FUTILITY OF AVOIDING CRITICISM

budget will stand" rather than on established and widely recognized bench marks of merit and advancement.

In the absence of any really tangible expressions of feedback, the church is too often silent, defaulting to other, lesser methods of evaluation. One of these is negative—measuring success by the absence or presence of criticism. In one church—I could count on it with absolute certainty—there was one person who always judged the success of an annual congregational meeting by "how smooth it went," meaning nobody got out of line. This comment always left me with mixed thoughts because I felt the meetings were perfunctory and lifeless. It is illusory to use lack of criticism as a measure of how you are doing.

Myth: A New Start Will Be Different

When crisis-provoking criticism comes, we are likely to respond in three ways—to stand our ground and fight, to take flight, or to join the attacker in punishing ourselves. A stepped-up work pace, recitations of how busy we are, and compulsive record-keeping of personal activities indicate a fight attitude, an attempt at self-justification. On the other hand, indulging in fantasies of moving to a new church and starting all over again is normal flight behavior.

Each is a way of coping with the pain of criticism. Each is limited, however, in its growth potential because it keeps us from facing the truth about ourselves. Changing jobs and geography is one way to separate ourselves from unpleasantries, but it has limited problem-solving potential. We do little more than exchange one set of problems for another—criticism in one area will be replaced by negative messages in another.

Of course, starting again in a different work setting will provide challenges, new testings of our abilities and skills, and opportunities to learn from past failures. It won't shield you from the bogey man of criticism.

Myth: Criticism Must Be Avoided

The optimum situation in ministry is not the absence of criticism, a situation in which church people are in total agreement with everything the minister does or says. This would be indeed a dull, apathetic church. Rather, criticism adroitly analyzed and applied can contribute to our self-learning and growth. This is not to minimize its stresses and its hurts. Disapproving, negative feedback is difficult to take at best. When it is followed by hostile, angry feelings, it stimulates all our primitive, self-protective energies, not the least of which is our fight/flight responses.

When criticism comes, the central issue is not "How can you get away from it?" but "How can you learn from it?" Your answer will largely determine what impact it will have on you, whether it will lead to growth-enhancing change or crisis-provoking withdrawal.

As you confront a particular criticism for the first time, ask yourself these questions, allowing the answers to put you in touch with yourself.

- How do you feel about yourself at the moment?
- Does the criticism focus on what you believe to be an inadequacy?
- What is being criticized? If it centers on one of the roles of ministry, ask yourself how invested are you in that role; that is, what threatens you most by the criticism?
- What is your past track record with negative messages?
- How sensitive are you to the criticism potential in others?
- How does this affect your self-disclosing in relationships?

Chapter 4
Trusting Your Feelings

Our feelings relate what is alive, real, and spontaneous within to people, things, and events around us. They energize our actions. Feelings are our very life—at times down, uncomfortable, confused, sad, and discontented. But they also reflect moments—more than we realize—when we're comfortable, excited, surprised, glad, and proud.

Hostile blaming is an intrusion on our feelings. Traumatic personal assaults and demeaning put-downs often come randomly and unexpectedly. Persons with whom we have had a previously meaningful relationship, overcome with disappointment and anger, may choose to dump on us their resentment and hostility at the slightest irritation. Feeling hurt, they may wish to hurt. Whatever the precipitating reason for the faultfinding, it is painful to be accused of incompetence and failure to measure up to the critic's expectations. Clergy seem to be particularly vulnerable to unanticipated, random hostility.

George Bach and Herb Goldberg point to recent studies that show that experienced psychiatrists have more difficulty than young intern therapists in dealing with anger directed at themselves from patients. Furthermore, they say, therapists tend to avoid patients who are openly hostile toward them.[1] Even when anger is encouraged during therapy by highly skilled doctors, it is an emotionally draining experience on doctor as well as patient.

POTSHOTS AT THE PREACHER

How clergy react to such stress and struggle for emotional equilibrium is the subject of this chapter.

Think back to the last time you felt stomach-knotting criticism. Do you recall where you were, the physical setting? Can you describe feelings before and during the criticism event? What tensions and weaknesses did you feel in your body? A tightening, tensing sensation in your chest? An ebbing, empty feeling in your stomach? A momentary flush in your face and a tingling in the back of your scalp? Were you aware of a slight quiver in your voice as you struggled for self-control?

Recently, I discovered how powerful even veiled criticism can be in smoking out feelings. This time I took the role of critic, although during the course of the day the role shifted. For several years I had been meeting regularly with a small group of clergy and mental-health professionals. On this particular morning several of us had driven nearly fifty miles to the meeting. It seemed like all the others—the same faces, and nothing very exciting about the agenda. Without admitting the disappointment I felt, I suggested to the group that they should expand their membership to include new people and hopefully some new ideas.

There was consensus. Nevertheless, John—a friend sitting across from me and a founder of the group—appeared to withdraw from the conversation. In the thirteen years he and I had been friends, he usually invested himself fully in every group of which he was a part. I personally valued his talents as a hospital chaplain and clinical pastoral-education teacher.

Adjourning before noon, those of us who had traveled together in my car went to lunch. John remained quiet during the meal. On the trip home, he sat in the rear with Mike, his co-worker at the mental-health institute. We had been driving

TRUSTING YOUR FEELINGS

for about half an hour when John called from the rear: "Jim, what do you really want this committee to do?"

I sensed the irritation in his voice. Before I could answer, he asked: "Do you remember when you as chairman of the synod committee [a committee John and I had worked on together] made some decisions without consulting the rest of us?" I felt embarrassed that my friend of long standing would raise an issue more than five years old in front of the others.

The other two passengers turned their attention toward us. Trained pastoral counselors, they did not intervene or try to divert the mounting heat. Secretly, I hoped they would. We arrived at the institute, but before we bid good-bye, John invited me to his office for coffee. I quickly declined, saying I had to get back to some work. Feeling uneasy as I drove away, I knew John was angry; we had not resolved what clearly had become a problem between us. I had been in my office for less than an hour when the telephone rang. It was John: "Jim, I apologize for gunnysacking you in the car this afternoon."

"That's all right," I stammered.

"No, let me finish," he continued. "I felt shocked and hurt by what you said in the meeting this morning. I took your comments personally because I've invested so much in that group over the years. When Mike and I got back to the office, he helped me to see how I was putting my hurt onto you."

During the next few moments we were able to talk and resolve the issue. Just reflecting together briefly about the day and sharing our bad feelings helped us to heal our wounds and move on to talk of other things.

Repressed Feelings, Role Feelings, and Real Feelings

Repressed Feelings. Rather than admit them to yourself, much less to another person, it is easier to repress feelings.

POTSHOTS AT THE PREACHER

People who have been through a criticism event frequently describe being shocked, hurt, and angry. Sometimes they will report being criticized, but will either dilute its importance or deny their feelings. This is dangerous. Repressing feelings only drives the energy further under the surface. It's like trying to push a floating ball under water. The bigger the ball, the harder it is to submerge. When you let go, it is forcefully thrust to the surface by the pressure of the water beneath.

Role Feelings. In addition, clergy, spouses, or members of religious orders are sometimes trapped by their role feelings. We express what we think is appropriate to our roles rather than how we feel. Role feelings give the appearance that we are calm, cool, listening, and communicative. But this is little more than playacting for the sake of personal security, reinforced by many years of conditioning.

As I reflect on my dialogue with John in the car, I met his hurt with self-protective responses. I did not want to be viewed by our companions as having acted unwisely or incompetently. Consequently, John had to make the second effort to catch my attention.

Role feelings that gloss over our true emotions act as barriers to effective interpersonal communication. Instead of communicating "in the moment" feelings, we interrupt ourselves with hidden "oughts" and "shoulds." We are more concerned about how we'll appear to others than with how we are communicating. Clark Moustakas writes:

> The individual stops trusting his own feelings and, since he cannot actually make another's feelings his own, he learns mechanically or automatically to make the proper gestures or facial expressions to denote the appropriate feelings; a smile is not a smile, joy is not joy, and sadness is not sadness; the movements of the face and body are properly placed to take on the appearance of appropriate emotions.[2]

TRUSTING YOUR FEELINGS

Real Feelings. We are in touch with our real feelings when our words and actions match how we feel inside. When we can be honest with ourselves and others, when "we can tell it like it is," then our real feelings are coming through.

Whose idea is it that clergy, wives or husbands of clergy, priests, and nuns should *always* be nice? Who said that persons "ordained of God" should set aside their humanity, not get angry, and stay cool under all conditions?

Criticism and Grief

There are striking similarities between natural losses in life, such as death and separation, and diminishment of self-esteem through criticism. Gregory Rochlin says that to lose someone we love or to lose our own self-esteem is likely to be the hardest blow that life deals us. In the dissolution of a meaningful relationship, he continues, a satisfying image of the self tends in part to be given up.[3] Dr. Rochlin believes that the self, when demeaned, produces conflicts and responses similar to those experienced through grief through other losses.

The grieving process is characterized by three phases—the initial impact phase, the recoil phase, and the recovery phase.

The Impact Phase

I spoke recently with a clergy couple from the South who described their first shock and dismay when a friend unloaded blaming criticism on them. Bill, who had executive responsibilities for the district, did not preach regularly but attended the local church with his family. One evening Bill and Barbara picked up a close friend, a member of the church they attended, and drove to a Bible class in a nearby town. "All at once," Barbara said, "our friend let us have it—all the hostility and venom that she'd been saving. She accused us of

POTSHOTS AT THE PREACHER

undermining the work of the local pastor. . . . We couldn't believe it; we were shocked, hurt, and wanting to say a lot of things we couldn't!"

Everett Shostrom says that when we feel hurt, which is difficult for most of us to express adequately, we become withdrawn and regressive. It is as if we want to act like a baby; we feel like crying.

Instead of letting tears come naturally and uninterrupted, which is embarrassing if you feel you should have your emotions under control, you may feel a sinking sensation in the pit of the stomach, increase in heart rate, and shortness of breath. In exchanging words, your own voice sounds hollow and suspended from the body. A wave of numbness insulates you from the hostile bombardment. Body and injured spirit struggle for reintegration.

Think back to the last time you felt hurt by someone's negative, critical accusation. Were you prepared, or did it take you by surprise? Like unexpected bad news, the critical confrontation usually catches us by surprise and shocks our whole being, leaving us feeling inadequate. It is the surprise element that compounds the initial shock and momentarily immobilizes us. Bill and Barbara, anticipating a pleasant evening with good friends, were caught by surprise. What happened to the trust between them and their critical friend? "Why has she done this to us?" they thought.

The surprise quality of most criticism often reinforces our feeling of being responsible for the alleged mistake. Because the criticism may have a kernel of truth in it and the person who is giving it is significant to us, we may conclude, "My gosh, I'm guilty. I've been found out," or "I should have been on time; I don't have any excuse." At the moment of impact, the "shoulds" and the "oughts" flood our consciousness, and we begin to feel responsible, guilty, and ashamed.

TRUSTING YOUR FEELINGS

Henri Nouwen, the sensitive Merton-like guru of contemplation and spiritual formation, reveals his own difficulty in coping with criticism:

> I hardly remember what it was, but a small critical remark and a few irritations during my work in the bakery were enough to tumble me head over heels into a deep, morose mood. Many hostile feelings were triggered and in a long sequence of morbid associations, I felt worse and worse about myself, my past, my work, and all the people who came to mind. But happily I saw myself tumbling and was amazed how little was needed to lose my peace of mind and to pull my whole world out of perspective. Oh, how vulnerable I am![4]

A person, acutely fearful of rejection and disapproval, may be most vulnerable to hurt at the initial impact of criticism. If self-concept is built solely on acceptance by others, the impact phase may include traces of shock, numbness, and disbelief.

The person whose self-esteem is generally intact still feels the sting of faultfinding, but recovers more rapidly.

The Recoil Phase

In spite of the initial stress, daily responsibilities continue. Sermons have to be written, meetings attended, clothes washed, garbage carried out, and classes prepared. Between all the "have tos" and "want tos" you reconstruct what you could have said and done. Intentional and random thoughts alike invade consciousness without any effort.

Can you identify the kinds of fantasies that whirled in and out of your mind following the last hurtful event? How prominent were the flight thoughts, "We'll move to another parish," or the fight fantasies, "I'll hurt you as much as you've hurt me"?

Such involuntary thoughts, the sorting out of conflicting

feelings, are part of the grieving process during this recoil phase. Let's look at some of them.

Angry Feelings. Persons in the religious vocation are often fearful of anger. Being angry with a person may be viewed as contradictory to religious teaching. It is all right to denounce social injustices, but it is not acceptable to be hostile and resentful toward other people, especially if they are your parishioners.

Angry feelings readily flow from criticism events, observable in the hostile critic as well as in your emotional response. After the first shock, angry feelings undoubtedly are present, though you may not recognize them as such. Instead, you may feel sad, unhappy, or unexcited about your daily activities.

According to Leo Madow, angry feelings may be so repressed we are unaware of them. He cites a number of clues that signal the presence of hidden anger. Among them are altered speech patterns, passive behavior visible in the silent treatment, sarcastic humor, forgetting an appointment or promise, excessive niceness, and mild forms of depression.

Furthermore, Dr. Madow has discovered a strong correlation between repressed anger and accidents. The fast, impatient driver speeding home from work may be unaware of anger toward the boss or co-workers. In addition, references to "organ language"—such as "I couldn't stomach him!"—are a way of communicating anger.

Unrecognized anger, if allowed to stay submerged, can contribute to physical disability. As our bodies prepare for stress, excess energy builds up in our sympathetic nervous system and mobilizes forces to meet stress. Secretions of blood sugar and adrenalin increase the heart rate and blood pressure. If such physical energy is not appropriately discharged, it can be physically harmful.[5]

Those "Blah" Feelings. People react differently under

TRUSTING YOUR FEELINGS

stress. Some are stimulated to greater activity; others in the days and weeks following some precipitous criticism event may experience a lack of enthusiasm for simple tasks, such as getting out of bed in the morning. Persons who have sustained the sudden loss of a family member report "having lost interest in life." It may be that if we have experienced a blow to our self-esteem—a humiliation, a dejection, an overt expression of our unworthiness—we may become depressed.

Feeling blue or down in the dumps may include being tired upon rising in the morning, loss of appetite, diminishment of sexual interest, and feelings of hopelessness. We may not feel very good about what we are doing or about ourselves. Work becomes routine, even boring. Reluctant to commit ourselves to anything in the future that requires creativity or effort, we may be troubled by waves of panic that increase our sense of being immobilized.

Depressive symptoms are usually so uncomfortable that you may be frightened by what seems to be a lack of control over your world. Such fear results from feeling powerless to cope with the criticism, the critic, or the uncomfortable physical symptoms. Add to this feelings of guilt, and you are likely to ask, "What is wrong with my faith? Why am I unable to pull myself together?"

If feeling that life has lost its zest is a new experience for you, it is probably temporary. But if this feeling persists over any extended period, don't suffer alone; share your pain with a close friend or counselor.

The Recovery Phase

You eventually reach the recovery period in the due course of grief work. During this phase a person begins to let go of the past—its pain and loss—and direct energies toward the future. It means rebuilding broken relationships, if that is possible, or letting go of them if they are beyond repair. Letting go of the past is a positive, take-charge-of-your-own-life action. Instead of letting events and situations control you—a passive response—you test your own sense of power.

Moving in this direction, ask yourself: "What am I learning about my own ability or inability to handle criticism?" Of the six factors identified in chapter 2, which seem to explain your sensitivity to criticism?

Perhaps the most difficult part of recovery is honestly and candidly facing the truth as well as the falseness of criticism. If it is an attack upon you personally, is there something in how you relate to people that results in mixed messages? For example, do you speak about closeness and openness in relationships, but by gestures, eye contact, and voice tone communicate distance and superiority?

If the criticism has been directed toward a particular skill of ministry—that is, preaching, administration, educational leadership, or some phase of pastoral care—you may still take it personally. Nevertheless, check how you are feeling with the six factors through which persons may perceive criticism. How much of your own needs are you projecting onto the criticism and the critic? It is important to differentiate clearly the target of the criticism. In other words, if through criticism you learned you made a mistake, admit it and go on from there.

Experience Your Feelings

There is more to experiencing feelings than just talking about them. Experiencing our emotions, according to the Gestalt view, is tuning in on the here and now—becoming aware of our body gestures, breathing, feelings, voice tone, and facial expressions. It is taking hold of the present and

TRUSTING YOUR FEELINGS

exercising the right of ownership that being in the here and now offers.

Gestalt, derived from an untranslatable German word, views the person as a total human being who experiences life in patterns and wholes rather than in compartments or segments. A reaction to older, traditional theories of behavior, Gestalt believes we cannot get along in the present unless we learn how to engage every moment to its fullest potential, including the problems that we encounter along the way. Unlike other therapies preoccupied with past events, Gestalt concentrates on helping a person identify his own means of psychological support.[6]

Fritz Perls, Gestalt's leading interpreter, says that if a person can become truly aware of himself on whatever level—fantasy, verbal, or physical—he can see what his present difficulties are and can work to solve them in the present.

A concept that has important implications for persons in the religious vocation is what Perls calls "self-interruption." To interrupt uncomfortable thoughts and feelings prevents total participation in the present. The common headache, according to Perls, can be a mechanism for interrupting the normal flow of emotion. Instead of being open about skepticism or distrust, it is easier to have a headache.

The self-interruptor, if a minister, priest, or religious, may have learned early in life to suppress certain thoughts, actions, feelings, and intentions, believing them to be unworthy or even sinful. In choosing a "holy" life, the self-interruptor chose not to allow himself or herself to have thoughts and feelings that would be counter to that first commitment. In some instances this is reinforced by parents and elders who project their own expectations of how one going into the religious life should behave.

A Roman Catholic nun, who is a leader in her order,

POTSHOTS AT THE PREACHER

recently shared her self-interrupting feelings and behavior resulting from what she described as a warm and supportive relationship with a teacher at a neighboring university. She wrote:

> I was immediately judged when phone calls came to the house and Brother came for a visit. I immediately shifted gears and made arrangements to meet him at other places than our grounds. This gave me guilt feelings and also the fear of being seen, etc.; but the fact that I was really cared for and important was a greater feeling than the criticism. . . . He became an extremely important person in my life.

In this instance an obviously beautiful relationship was kept private, preventing it from the freedom and spontaneity that it deserved.

Our self-interrupting mechanisms may seduce us into behaviors that value "public relations" more than spontaneity. After a busy day I would have liked a beer at one of the local pubs in the small town where I first served as a minister. But the highly moralistic expectations expressed by influential parishioners reinforced my need to earn their respect, and so I never went into any of the town's taverns. Since a significant part of the community's social life centered around the churches and the taverns, on reflection I wonder how many opportunities for ministry I may have missed.

The following are some commonsense suggestions for opening your emotional channels during times of stress.

Identify What Is Happening to You

We have all observed persons walking down the street talking and smiling to themselves, preoccupied and oblivious to pedestrians and other distractions of the street. Dialoguing with yourself is one way to get in touch with your feelings.

TRUSTING YOUR FEELINGS

Fritz Perls suggests several questions that a person can ask of one's self to monitor inner processes. The next time you feel that you are in a stressful situation—the next time you are with a person who's angry with you—ask of yourself: What are you doing? What are you feeling? What are you wanting? What are you avoiding? What are you expecting? The cause of the stress probably won't go away or diminish, but you will know what's happening to you and hopefully will accept it as *you* in the situation. Answers may not come easily, but it will be a beginning toward assuming responsibility for how you feel during times of joy as well as stress.

Go with Your Predominant Feelings

This is another way of saying, Know how you feel and let yourself go with that feeling for a while. Feel the hot flush in your face and the dry, pasty coating in your mouth. Or feel the tenseness in your muscles, a pulling at the back of your neck. Admit that you are angry, at least to yourself, so that you can be more comfortable with the emotion.

It is possible that you may experience the tension before you can identify the feeling. If you are troubled by a persistent drawing of muscles in any part of your body, reflect on what has been happening to you. Look for irritations and conflicts in some of your primary relationships.

For example, instead of pushing back your anger at being criticized, recognize it, admit it to yourself—verbally if possible—and live with it so that you are more comfortable with this feeling. Find out where and how anger hides itself in your body. Learn where the tension mounts. Discover what is uniquely you as you feel your anger.

A Wisconsin researcher, Leonard Berkowitz, cautions against "letting it all hang out" with the target of your anger when discharging bottled-up feelings. Such aggression only leads to more aggression with less inhibitions. Instead of meeting a verbal attack (an aggressive act) with a counter-attack (an aggressive and defensive act), Berkowitz argues for reporting your anger to let the other person know how he has affected you.[7] This, he feels, has a more satisfying therapeutic impact on both parties.

Living with an emotion helps get it out where we can look at it, feel it, and accept it. Emotions are our enemies only when we fear them or allow them to have free reign without any restraints.

Accept and Appropriately Discharge Your Feelings

Pleasurable, exhilarating emotions are often taken for granted. We accept them without much thought; sometimes we wish we could sustain them for longer periods. Uncomfortable, troublesome feelings are more difficult to manage. They irritate and frustrate. They can waste valuable energy in self-defeating and self-protecting activity. Consider these ways of accepting and discharging your feelings.

Thinking Out Loud. Sometimes it helps to think about what is going on with someone else—a trusted friend, maybe even your spouse. In order for thinking out loud to be helpful, be clear with the other person about what you expect his or her role to be. If you want advice, indicate that at the beginning. It may not be advice you want at all; rather you may want someone who will be an active listener and who will help you to clarify what it is you're feeling. Active listening is not only hearing the other's words, but it involves tuning into the intensity or passivity of feeling behind those words. It is not only listening to the sound of your voice, but also the silences. The active listener is likely to ask clarifying questions such as, "What are you meaning to say by that?" or "Could you say that another way?"

TRUSTING YOUR FEELINGS

If you feel the stress is getting out of hand, you may want to seek out a professional counselor—a member of your community mental-health center, a private psychotherapist, a pastoral counselor, or a specialist in career development. Most denominational health plans provide limited psychiatric counseling for clergy families. Fortunately, a variety of career-evaluation services are available to those in the religious vocation. Sometimes, all that is necessary to gain inner equilibrium is an opportunity to reflect on the experiences with a trained observer. Many who have been through career evaluation report they have been reaffirmed as persons and as professionals. Personal reflection and setting goals stimulate growth and maturity.

Recreation. Edgar Jackson, whose books on grief work are required reading for seminarians, advocates regular exercise to maintain muscle tone and cardiovascular health.[8] This is especially important when you are under stress, for when vessels contract, blood pressure rises. Bicycling, jogging, vigorous walking, and swimming are particularly good for the cardiovascular system and should be sustained for at least forty-five minutes three times a week. If you've been sedentary for any time, it is wise to undergo a thorough physical examination before engaging in strenuous exercise.

Do you take at least one day a week off to be with your family, putter around the house, play golf, fish, take your spouse to lunch, or do just what you want to do? Better still, do you take off two days, including Saturday and Sunday afternoons when the kids are home? Recreational diversions will not make your problems disappear, but they will keep you from making your work a seven-day-a-week obsession. If you don't take a regular day off, ask yourself why. Compulsion to work may be your way of resolving guilt feelings.

Continuing Education. Where did ministers get the notion

that it is selfish or improper for persons called of God to take care of their own physical, emotional, intellectual, and spiritual health? I have known clergy who put their work before all else, including family, health, and just plain common horse sense. All work or all play soon becomes burdensome; the first blush of exhilaration waxes pale if you have too much of any one experience. If you are given to workaholism, continuing education may serve a useful purpose in temporarily putting distance between you and your work. Sometimes it is just refreshing to get away from the demands and routines of the parish to participate in the emotional and intellectual stimulation that a continuing-education event may offer.

More frequent is the function of continuing education in building authentic personal–professional competence, which influences how we feel about ourselves. With increased self-esteem comes a renewed sense of our own personal authority. With enhanced self-esteem, we will less likely feel vulnerable to criticism and, hopefully, will be less deserving of it.

There is no shortage of opportunities; in fact, some complain that there are too many, which makes choosing difficult. Seminaries, state universities, clinical pastoral-education centers, and private agencies offer a wide scope of programs to meet just about any need or interest. Fortunately, there are a variety of offerings ranging from doctor of ministry programs that require substantial time and financial commitments to short courses of one to five days or more. Choose the style and form that best suits you. Here are some examples:

1. In-parish: non-academic. This includes reading, study using tapes, and reflection. Several hours each week spent in this kind of learning are a normal part of your

TRUSTING YOUR FEELINGS

schedule. With the congregation you can create ways to learn together so that you are not alone in trying to meet all the church's needs. Cost is negligible.
2. In-parish: academic. Correspondence courses and seminars taken at nearby colleges and seminaries involve little travel or time away from home or work. Some programs may lead to advanced degrees. Cost varies.
3. Out-of-parish: professional. Emphasis is upon the learning and practicing of skills, theory, and personal growth. Training may be at a hospital, institution, or center, and time away from work may range from three days to twelve weeks in residence. Cost varies.[9]

Since the congregation makes time available for continuing education, and in some instances the funds, it is sometimes prudent to include the board as you begin to plan. Mutual discussion may help to establish a long-term plan for your continuing education as well as congregational commitment to it. [10]

Spiritual Renewal. Thomas R. Kelly, a Quaker mystic and life-long student of the devotional life, writes:

> Deep within all there is an amazing inner sanctuary of the soul, a holy place, a Divine Center, a speaking Voice, to which we may continuously return. Eternity is at our hearts pressing upon our time-torn lives, warming us with intimations of an astounding destiny, calling us home unto Itself. . . . What is here urged are internal practices and habits of the mind . . . ways of conducting our inward life so that we are perpetually bowed in worship while we are also very busy in the world of daily affairs.[11]

Clergy who have daily and weekly worship responsibilities may be neglecting their own spiritual development. Do you

POTSHOTS AT THE PREACHER

schedule a regular daily quiet time just to think, pray, or meditate?

You may not be able to take other than a leadership role most Sundays, but consider worshiping periodically at a neighboring church, during a weekday prayer service, for example. Visit the retreat centers in your area and get to know the retreat directors. Take a meal at the center, participate in the worship, and perhaps visit the library. You'll be most welcome.

None of these activities will ward off criticism or shield you from its hurt. Hopefully, you will return to your desk refreshed in both body and spirit.

Thinking out loud, recreation, continuing education, and spiritual renewal are a few ways of accepting yourself and paying attention to yourself. Acceptance not only begins when we see other people as if they have a right to be themselves, but when we accept our right to be ourselves. Self-acceptance, says Jess Lair, is like peeling an onion. "You get off one layer of acceptance of feelings and thoughts and ideas and problems, and then all you've got is another layer underneath. You keep on working on that all your life, seeing new paths for yourself, new areas that need acceptance." [12]

Chapter 5
Why Criticism Comes

Criticism comes to a person for one or two reasons: (1) he or she has made a mistake or is so perceived, or (2) some stress in the life of the critic is acted out in the form of faultfinding. Chapter 8 will focus primarily on valid criticism and how it can be expressed in the church. In this chapter I explore some common stresses of life that may be overlooked in the heat of confrontation but that may generate the energy behind very severe and punitive negativism.

When news leaked out that the worship committee planned to make some changes in the arrangement of candles on the communion table, Aunt Tillie's nephew John was understandably exercised and complained to his pastor. He explained how he and his family had given the candles as a memorial to Aunt Tillie fifteen years ago, and he didn't think anyone had a right to tamper with them. He pointed his finger at the minister and shouted, "It's your fault; since you've come to this congregation, we've lacked sound leadership from the pulpit."

He continued, "This church used to be known for its biblical preaching. We're sadly lacking it now! People are leaving the church because of it."

Suppose you were John's minister. What would you be feeling? Is his charge true? How would you respond? You may not know what John is feeling, but you do know what he is saying. He's upset, angry, frustrated, and he has chosen you to be the target of his feelings.

Hold on! The issue may not be you or your alleged incompetencies. The problem may be with John—a particularly troublesome stress that he's acting out with you. Some of the possibilities might be—

1. unresolved anger;
2. changes in life-situation;
3. frustration in relationships;
4. dissatisfaction with church work.

Unresolved Anger

Flip Wilson's brash, egotistical *femme fatale* Geraldine says to her imaginary boyfriend, Killer: "What you sees, Honey, is what you gets!" But not everyone is as immediately transparent and self-revealing as Geraldine, especially within the church setting. There is a lot of under-the-surface stuff that never really gets communicated until the explosion, and then it is too late. The battle lines have been drawn and attitudes polarized. Like the patient who feels pain but is afraid to go to the doctor until it gets unbearable, some parishioners hold their anger and resentment inside or express them only indirectly.

When this backlog of emotion does erupt it may come without warning and at the slightest provocation. Here are two ways researchers are looking at hidden anger.

Masked Depression

An emotionally explosive person, according to psychiatrist Stanley Lesse, may be depressed without really identifying feelings as such.[1] Instead of being a means of venting and

WHY CRITICISM COMES

relieving the depression, rage actually masks it. The rage becomes a vehicle for trying to ward it off.

Another clinical facet of masked or hidden depression is how anger gets discharged. When it focuses on inappropriate targets within the family setting, the person with masked depression may shout at his wife and nag at the children for something that is more a problem at the office than at home. It is easier to attack a safe, available target than to be angry with the boss who can fire you, the secretary who can ignore you, or the custodian who might tell you off.

The person with symptoms of masked depression, feeling a sense of power mixed with vindictiveness, probably thinks: "Now you will feel the power of my anger and my actions! No one cares how I suffer, so why should I care if anyone else suffers?" In observing and treating hundreds of patients, Lesse has identified some distinguishing characteristics: Persons with symptoms of masked depression are usually above average in intelligence and have high expectations of themselves. They are not satisfied with second best and aggressively try to dominate their environment. Critical of others, they are sometimes overbearing and controlling. Potential friends are put off by their actions. Their need to dominate the environment, says Lesse, is an attempt to compensate for lifelong feelings of inadequacy and self-depreciation.

As a parish pastor working with persons of all kinds, you may be the target for hostility that rightfully belongs elsewhere. Listen and be sensitive to clues that may point to a larger problem.

Crazymaking

George Bach and Herb Goldberg have introduced the idea of "crazymaking" as another way of describing how some persons handle their pent-up rage.[2] Crazymaking is an interpersonal transaction in which there is a crazymaker and an object (a victim or sufferer). Crazymaking behavior confuses the victim in its unpredictability and oscillation between ingratiating charm and raging hate. The crazymaker hides his inner anger by being excessively nice. This concept may explain how some clergy and parishioners relate to one another; in some instances the minister or priest takes on the role of crazymaker. As previously stated, persons in religious occupations have particular difficulty recognizing and discharging their anger and hide their hostility behind excessive kindness.

Whether they be clergy or laity, Bach and Goldberg note that crazymakers can be identified by one or more of the following behaviors.

Gives Confusing Messages. "In very short order and for the seemingly pettiest of reasons they oscillate from expressions of concern, caring, tenderness, and love to critical, rejecting, punitive, and even insulting outbursts." The researchers cite the parent who is expansive and loving one day, sullen and withdrawn the next. Is this any different from behavior we observe at some parish board and committee meetings? One day the crazymaker reaches out toward you and the next is pushing you away. You never know quite how to meet or touch such a person. How do you relate to the fluctuating moods? More important, you aren't sure it's worth the risk.

Makes Impossible Requests. Demands for perfection are so unrealistic that, according to Bach and Goldberg, "the victim invariably winds up feeling inadequate; nothing he or she does is ever really good enough."

A few years ago a young woman in her early twenties walked into my office and asked if she could talk with me; her grandmother in another city had died, and she felt bad that she couldn't get back for the funeral. She said she just wanted to

WHY CRITICISM COMES

talk with me about her grandmother. After an hour or so, she asked me to have prayer with her and left. A couple of weeks later on a Sunday morning before service, she telephoned to say she had broken up with her boyfriend. Then she made an interesting request.

"Would you go over to his apartment and take back what belongs to me?" she asked.

I said I couldn't do this, but I offered to meet with her that day to talk about it. Without further word, she hung up. About a month later she called again and angrily explained how she had tried to commit suicide, was hospitalized, and had just been released.

"If you'd done what I asked of you, this never would have happened!" (a crazymaking accusation). With that, she slammed down the receiver, and I never saw or heard from her again. I felt terrible for days after that. But I also felt I had followed my best judgment, though the result was not what I had hoped.

As this anecdote illustrates, it is difficult to head off crazymaking since the crazymaker sees his or her behavior differently. Whether intentional or not, the person sets up the situation so that any confrontation is viewed as an impugnation of the highest motives.

Needs Your Dependence. Overprotective and concerned beyond reason, the crazymaker treats the other person as a child. Sometimes an entire congregation gets into this stance with its minister. Because of gifts, favors, gratuities, and special considerations, the pastor is perpetually being grateful about something. The withholding of these favors, or the perceived threat that they might be withheld, is an effective controlling mechanism.

One very old and once prestigious congregation had an unusual relationship with its ministers. They accorded inordinate courtesy to the senior pastor who had been with them more than twenty-five years, virtually ignoring the other staff. At one rather ordinary parish dinner I observed parishioners scurrying about to make sure the senior pastor had the honored place at the head table. The young assistant and his wife had to fend for themselves. Youthful ministers in that church came and went in rapid succession, some leaving in the midst of intense personal criticism.

But in spite of this gross inequity the congregation took care of its favorite preacher, as I learned one Sunday when I conducted service during his absence. Arriving about an hour early, I was ushered to a small, well-appointed room complete with private bath and a large vibrator chair. This, the custodian explained, was to help Doctor _____ relax before the service. Within a few minutes, a woman, who I judged to be in her late fifties, appeared at the door with a tray of milk and cookies.

"The Reverend always has refreshment before he preaches," she said. (I learned later that he had an ulcer.)

When I declined, she looked disconsolate and insisted on helping me into my pulpit gown. I'll never forget her parting remark: "We always take care of our Doctor _____."

Who knows what was closeted behind this conspiracy of niceness? The congregation and senior minister kept the fantasy that everything was O.K., while the youthful associates lived in the real world and took on the misappropriated hostility resulting from everything not being O.K. If crazymaking is to be successful, says Bach and Goldberg, everyone caught in its web must cooperate:

> Even though crazymaking ultimately proves very destructive to its victims, causing extreme detachment, instability, overdependency, chronic anxiety, and even breakdown, the victim's poor self-image and deep feelings of inadequacy tend to cause him to

WHY CRITICISM COMES

cling to the crazymaking relationship and to view it as a critical, life-sustaining involvement.[3]

Changes in Life-Situation

There may be a correlation between hostile faultfinding in the church and how the parishioner-critic is presently experiencing life. When a person is so frustrated and upset that he explodes at a board meeting or other semipublic occasion, look for change-oriented factors in that person's life.

For years researchers have been fascinated with how change affects us. In the early thirties, researchers in Austria analyzed hundreds of life stories and theorized that most lives are marked by particular stages. They concluded that the earlier stages of life are characterized by an expansion of activities and dimensions, while the latter part has more negative changes such as sickness, loss of associates, and death of relatives.[4]

More recently Raymond Kuhlen found that frustration over life-changes may be a key motivational factor in adult psychology. One of the leading threats that adults face, he says, is the frustration that a person suffers because of a felt inability to do anything about life's circumstances, that is, feeling locked into a life-style.[5] He also found that sensitivity to changing time perspectives created anxiety. At some point in middle age we realize that time is running out, and our options are narrowing.

T. H. Holmes and R. H. Rahe have charted the emotional impact of forty-three life-situations on our emotional and physical health. They have measured how much change a person can experience and still stay relatively healthy. Using marriage as a base reference, they calculated the amount, severity, and duration of stress relative to getting married to be fifty points. Death of a spouse rated one hundred points and divorce rated seventy-three points. Going on vacation and Christmas rated thirteen points and twelve points respectively.

They also found that one significant change, such as death of a spouse, may lead to a number of other changes, thereby pushing the total toward the danger level of three hundred points.[6]

As every pastor knows only too well, much pastoral work revolves around helping people cope and adapt to changes. But undoubtedly there are some in your parish whose life-changes are not known to you until they drop out of church activities or become negative toward you or the church. By dropping out or being critical they get your attention. Then you may learn how circumstances are affecting their behavior.

Frustrations in Relationships

We are more likely to criticize another if there is tension in our relationship with that person. In a marriage, for example, strains in the relationship magnify even minor irritations. Resentments build over inadvertent slights when neither partner can fully please the other. When the tension builds to such stress that neither can tolerate it, one or both may stalk off to care for their wounds or fight it out until emotions are dissipated and the issues are resolved.

Unlike the physician who can treat a patient without being closely associated with that person, the minister has to depend upon relationships with parishioners as a vehicle for ministry. Your chief personal asset is your ability to relate and communicate with others. This ability is measured by statements such as: "Isn't Pastor Jones friendly?" "He seems to be so understanding." "I think I could tell him just about anything." "The young people like him."

WHY CRITICISM COMES

Some parishioners seek to be "extra special" with the minister or his family. They may be older persons who have discovered some elements of a son or daughter in you, or single persons who, feeling lonely and deprived of family, seek a parental-surrogate experience with your family. Frequently the overtures toward friendship are expressed directly through a variety of courtesies, gifts, and social invitations.

When parishioners who want to be particularly special feel put off or slighted, they may be jealous of any special attention you give to others. If you have a socially active relationship with a few people in your church, there may be some who feel disconsolate that they don't have this special friendship with you. They may have tried, but, for one reason or other, you did not encourage it. Father Donald Goergen has observed that "the jealous person is easily hurt because he needs to be the center of attention."[7]

If there is anything more difficult than managing your own dependency needs, it's handling the dependency that parishioners express toward you. All of us have dependency needs; none of us is completely self-sufficient all the time. Sometimes we need to support someone else during periods of crisis. The minister or priest accepts this as part of the task of pastoral care. But when a person's dependency seems insatiable, demanding, and possessive, you may recoil from it. In this process of drawing back, of putting distance between yourself and the dependent person, you risk criticism for being unfeeling or uncaring.

There will always be the possibility for criticism no matter how loving and caring and unselfish you are with your time. Since disappointment is a leading contributor to faultfinding, you risk failing others' expectations as you provide pastoral

POTSHOTS AT THE PREACHER

care. You will have fewer problems living with yourself if you just accept the risk as being part of your ministry.

Dissatisfaction with Church Work

People occasionally become resentful and critical when they are dissatisfied with the roles they have in the church. Role pressures—that is, the expectations that go with elected offices or with committee responsibilities—may not match the needs of those in the roles. Let us look at three sources of resentment that a person might experience within the church.[8]

Mismatched Roles and Personalities

People are at times recruited for the wrong tasks. For example, if a shy, reserved person is elected to the board of deacons, he or she may feel uncomfortable greeting visitors or calling on shut-ins and will eventually resent the task.

In one church, a young man with only an eighth-grade education was appointed church school teacher for a class of high-school students. The committee reasoned that his natural friendliness qualified him for the task. The recruiters appealed to his "Christian duty," and he took on the task. Before long both he and the students became restless and resentful of one another—he because the youth weren't paying attention, and they because he stayed too close to the teacher's book. One Sunday after class he quit, angrily accusing the education committee of not giving him enough support. He was probably right. He very likely felt inadequate in the assignment.

Contradictory Expectations in Roles

People are elected or appointed to tasks in the church but discover there are contradictions about what they are to do. A

WHY CRITICISM COMES

church school superintendent may be expected by some teachers to closely supervise their work, while others prefer to be left alone. Any attempt to be helpful is automatically suspect, so the person in this role feels frustration from the conflicting role expectations.

Contradictory expectation also arises when an individual attempts to fulfill two roles but finds the roles to be competitive. Board members usually serve as chairpersons of key committees in the church. If there are consuming tasks facing both the board and their committee, time becomes an issue: "How can I give the proper time to both jobs?" Role pressures may also arise at budget time when, as a board member, the individual is committed to a balanced budget but, as leader of the education committee, recommends expanding the educational program.

Sometimes these conflicting pressures—if caught early and aired—can be resolved; otherwise, resentments build and people resign or withdraw, blaming the minister, the board, and maybe even God for their frustrations.

Using Roles to Fulfill Personal Needs

Occasionally individuals seek positions of leadership in a church to meet personal needs. One involved parishioner once told me he felt guilty if he wasn't busy at the church. He rarely turned down a task unless he was going to be away at length on business.

Lacking status in their personal lives, some people find it in the church. Lay officers are ordained and installed, reflecting not only the respect of the whole church for the task, but the blessing of God as well. When candidates for such offices have not been adequately briefed before their election, a few soon discover there is more work than status, and they resign or drop away.

POTSHOTS AT THE PREACHER

Our needs are as much a part of us as our thoughts, our feelings, our hopes and dreams. When personal needs are not being met, or persons experience realities different from expectations, such discrepancies can lead to frustration and criticism.

Throughout most of this chapter I have discussed those painful outbursts of hostility and negativism that every parish pastor now and again experiences. When the emotional tone seems to outweigh the "offense," try to understand what is going on with the critic. This may not diminish your hurt feelings, but it may give some direction to your pastoral care of that person. Nevertheless, don't overlook the possibility that you have made a mistake, ignored a relationship, failed to fulfill a promise, or in one hundred other ways contributed to someone's disappointment. Hopefully you will be able to listen to and accept this legitimate feedback and resolve those problems that only you can resolve.

Chapter 6
The Super-Negative Critic

Is there someone in your parish who tests your patience with persistent, negative complaining? Do you have a parishioner or two who sets your agenda, keeps track of whether you are following it, and criticizes you when you don't? If you answered yes to both these questions, you join the legion of colleagues who have to contend with super-negative persons. Unlike those parishioners who offer valid, helpful criticism or even the person who is stressed by life's circumstances and is angry, the super-negative critic is chronically finding fault.

The behavior pattern is one consistent string of negatives. Like a toothache that won't quit, it is not life-threatening. But it hurts like hell! It doesn't make you sick, so you can't stay in bed. Instead, you go about your work constantly aware of the dull throb in your jaw. Just when you think the pain has subsided it jabs again.

Some people have a predilection for being hypercritical. When a new pastor comes, there will be a "honeymoon period" when even valid criticism is suppressed. But sooner or later the chronic complainer will test the new pastor's tolerance of criticism.

Super-negativism follows the Eric Berne model, "Now I've Got You, You S.O.B."[1] The accusing player takes an aggressive, parent role toward the other player who plays victim. As the game moves along, the aggressive player says, "I've been watching you, hoping you'd make a mistake."

Reacting with anxiety and guilt, the other player responds, "You caught me in a very stupid thing. I feel so humiliated. I won't do it again."

"Yes, and I'm going to let you feel the full force of my fury," retorts the first player, sensing the imbalance of power in the interpersonal transaction.

Let's look at an example. Barbara, a person whom I have admired over the years as being a conscientious, competent, and well-read minister, recently reported how impotent she felt when a board member, an antagonist of long standing, vociferously attacked her at a meeting. The critic focused on what he felt was a lack of parish calling on prospective new members. The attack followed some personal sharing in which Barbara expressed her concern about having to "moonlight" at a part-time denominational job to meet financial obligations. She had taken the job three years ago with the board's permission. During the outpouring of criticism (blaming Barbara for a variety of parish problems), the other board members withdrew into catatonic silence. Inside, she said, she felt angry and embarrassed but unable to "come up with anything" other than a few defensive arguments.

"I went home discouraged," Barbara continued, "because I felt I was alone in that meeting. The others let me take the full load. I have a need to please people; I guess I let this person set my agenda."

Barbara's situation is not unique, unfortunately. Too often clergy get pulled into Berne's "NIGYSOB" game because they are playing the "Super Minister Game." They communicate that they are larger than life—that they are able to take whatever anyone wants to throw their way. In short, when wounded they don't bleed. By repressing their own feelings of

THE SUPER-NEGATIVE CRITIC

anger because they feel it is unseemly for a minister to have them, they become the sacrificial lamb.

Some can manage this role, but others cannot. The cost is just too great to themselves, their families, and the church. As super-minister you communicate the message, "It's O.K. to kick me, I won't fight back." In effect this game does not resist manipulative and "put down" behavior. If you allow the chronic complainer to set your agenda, make first claim on your priorities, and drain your energies, your game is hooked into his. The feeling of powerlessness that can result may lead to depressive reaction.

Take Charge of the Moment

What are your options when an overly critical person criticizes you publicly before other parishioners? Returning to Barbara's situation, what could she have done to cope with the board member who was so accusatory toward her?

1. She could have defended herself with rebuttal to each point of the criticism. (This is in fact what she did, and she felt terrible.)
2. She could have walked out of the meeting.
3. She could have counterattacked, pointing out the weaknesses and mistakes of the critic.
4. She could have admitted her errors, apologized, and promised to do better.
5. She could have been direct with the person by sharing personal perceptions of the critic's actions and suggesting ground rules for dealing with the criticism.
6. She could have shared her own feelings with any of these.

POTSHOTS AT THE PREACHER

Since most criticism has some thread of truth to it, we are likely to react to it with guilt, even shame, if it stings hard enough. Particularly if the criticism is delivered with emotional impact, we are likely to be caught off guard, having to struggle with our own anxiety. It is within the first few moments of faultfinding that we either retreat into our usual coping/survival patterns or take charge of the moment by being assertive and direct.

A scenario that follows the fifth option might go something like this:

> *CRITIC:* This church isn't getting the attention it deserves from its pastor. New residents in the community are joining other churches because you don't visit them soon enough. You have time for everything else, but you're neglecting the church!
>
> *BARBARA:* I hear your criticism, and I also hear your anger, which seems to blame me when a new resident decides not to join our church.
>
> *CRITIC:* If you weren't so concerned about money, you wouldn't need to moonlight, and you'd have time for the church.
>
> *BARBARA:* I don't like the position you're putting me in; you're making me feel like a child who's being spanked by Mother. Besides, I think we need to clarify what the issues are.

In this scenario Barbara, listening carefully to the substance of the criticism as well as the emotional intent (she perceives it to be punishing), recovers enough from the initial shock to meet it head on, revealing some of her inner feelings. She not only listens to the other person's words, but observes the

THE SUPER-NEGATIVE CRITIC

feeling tone and her own inner reactions. Since the other members of the board are immobilized and silent, she takes full responsibility for reshaping the agenda.

Sometimes a person is so angry and blaming—boiling with emotion—all you can do is let the steam pop off. Let the emotion expend itself and then begin to sort out the issues.

The Compassion Trap

The super-minister may be involved in "the compassion trap" to avoid criticism. The vocation of ministry has a long history of being a compassion profession. In comparison to other occupations, monetary rewards are frequently modest. "Helping others" is the most frequently identified motivation for entering the ministry. Throughout the centuries the church has been viewed as a sanctuary that offered protection for the oppressed, retreat for the burdened, and alms for the needy. The minister/priest distributed goods and provided comfort for those seeking help. Persons could come at any time, day or night, ask for assistance, and receive it.

The compassion trap, conceptualized by Margaret Adams as being an exclusively female phenomenon, has implications for ministers.[2] It is the idea that a person exists to serve others, whatever the cost, and be on call around the clock to provide tenderness and compassion to all. Few could argue with the intent of such a lofty goal, but the trap is that in achieving the goal you may discount your own feelings and prior commitments. In brief, the compassion trap is a denial that you have feelings, priorities different from complete devotion to the needs of others, and physical as well as emotional limitations. The trap is believing that you can give when you no longer have anything to give, and if you give enough you will engender approval and gratitude.

POTSHOTS AT THE PREACHER

How would you respond to the following requests for your attention?

Situation One: The Disappointed Treasurer

Jack and his family are relatively new members of your church, having become active after many years of very nominal participation. Because Jack has been successful in business, the church board asked him to conduct the annual financial campaign to raise the church budget. He accepted the task and worked evenings and some weekends to prepare materials, meeting with the teams that would be visiting in each home.

Results of the campaign fell 25 percent short of the expected goal. Jack was perplexed. The church treasurer, a long-time member of the church, says to you angrily, "I told you Jack's fund-raising plan wouldn't work! If he hadn't insisted on letting the youth be part of the calling teams, we would have raised our budget. I'm going over to his home tonight and tell him just what I think of his program."

Instructions for individual study. Develop a short answer to each of the following questions:

1. What feelings can you identify in yourself?
2. What protective feelings do you have toward Jack?
3. What feelings do you have toward the treasurer?
4. How would you have responded to the treasurer's intention?

Situation Two: The Interrupted Birthday Party

Your daughter Beth has chosen to celebrate her seventeenth birthday with her parents and best friend at home. You have carefully planned for this event by scheduling meetings around it. During dinner the phone rings. It's Mrs. B____.

THE SUPER-NEGATIVE CRITIC

"Reverend Jones, I've been trying to get up the courage to call you all day. I'm so upset—I don't know what to do or who to turn to. I think my husband is having an affair. Could I see you tonight?"

Instructions for individual study. Develop a short answer to each question.
1. What feelings do you identify in yourself?
2. How would you respond to her request?
3. Is this similar to any real-life situations you have experienced? How did you cope?

In Situation One did you want to protect Jack from the treasurer's criticism? Would you try to restrain the treasurer by convincing him that such criticism might hurt Jack's feelings and possibly cause him to leave the church?

How about Situation Two? Would you have left the party to comply with Mrs. B——'s request? Of the two options before you for the remainder of the evening, which had priority? What conditions would alter that priority?

Avoiding the compassion trap does not mean that you care less about people or isolate yourself from their needs. It means redefining the meaning of compassion. Even Jesus did not try to meet every request. Occasionally he withdrew to a friend's home to recoup his strength. But when he was with a person who made claim upon him, he gave his whole attention.

When Jesus was asked by a scribe, "Which commandment is the first of all?" He replied that the first is "Love the Lord your God with all your heart, and with all your soul, and with all your mind, and with all your strength." He immediately followed it with the second commandment: "You shall love your neighbor as yourself" (Mark 12:30-31).

Jesus affirms the need for self-respect as a requisite for loving others. The Greek New Testament word for loving self, a form of agape, implies an acceptance and an affirmation of your own feelings, limitations, and strengths. Compassion toward your neighbor, according to Jesus, shall at least equal your own sense of self-worth. When you can accept yourself, implicit in agape, then you are free to relate to others out of the depth of your personal resources. By respecting yourself, your strengths and limitations, you can meet the other person on equal footing—person to person.

Renegotiate the Boundaries

When you attempt to cope with a highly critical person at a place and time that he or she has arbitrarily decided upon, then you are playing his or her game. You have been manipulated, either by your own anxiety or guilt, to settle the issue right then or there. The truth is that you may not have the energy or the time, or you may not think the occasion appropriate for such a discussion. If a person wants to criticize you at length for your sins you have the right to negotiate the turf. It doesn't have to be at the board meeting or the congregational meeting. If others take up the critic's banner, however, then you will have to cope with that issue at the time.

Sherod Miller, Elam Nunnally, and Daniel Wackman have outlined a procedure for managing misunderstandings in relationships, disagreements, and criticism. The procedure is based on the assumption that all parties to an issue or conflict or criticism count equally—there should be no one-upmanship or power moves.

1. What is the issue? It is important to know what you are discussing. But you have to be careful; sometimes the real issue is not the first one presented.

THE SUPER-NEGATIVE CRITIC

2. Whose issue is it? Barbara was being criticized for neglecting the parish by working at a second job. The real issue may be: Why must she work at a second job? Is the parish paying a fair salary? The issue is a church-wide concern, not just Barbara's problem.
3. Who is included? The answer to the above question will determine who is to be in on the discussion.
4. Where to talk? A public meeting may not be the most conducive place to talk. You do not have to deal with criticism solely on the critic's terms. Suggest a private face-to-face meeting if the issue is just between two of you.
5. When to talk? The hour of the day, your own schedule, and your energy level are factors when deciding on an appointment to talk.
6. How long to talk? Set a definite time and stick to it. Don't get trapped by your own need to keep the discussion going until you feel better or the complaint is resolved.[3]

Counseling both churches and clergy who were targets of disruptive tactics from both left and right extremists in the late sixties, Howard Clinebell wrote: "Experience indicates that a timid or indecisive approach, in the hope of avoiding controversy, is a type of appeasement. It encourages more demands."[4] The super-negative critic is a demanding person. Any legitimate criticism of church programs should be noted and evaluated. But when the negativism is based on false information, lack of evidence, and methods that disregard basic respect for people, it should be firmly resisted.

Patience, Clinebell says, can be interpreted as an invitation to manipulation and exploitation. Even during the most severe stress, be faithful in your pastoral work and administratively responsible in keeping the church going.

It is impossible for a creative person to avoid criticism. The overly negative person will always be around to introduce you to feelings and thoughts you didn't know you had. If you decide not to be manipulated—to play the persecutor–victim game—you can be direct with that person, call "stop action" to put-downs, and meet the person and his complaint head on. It may be painful, but you'll feel better the next morning.

Chapter 7
Criticism and the Minister's Wife

What is so unique about the role of clergy wife?[1] Is her role different from a doctor's spouse, a teacher's wife, or even a farmer's wife? We cannot point to the obvious clergy attributes—busyness, evenings away from home, preferential status in the community. Many breadwinners work at jobs with hours equal to or exceeding the minister's; many are gone during the week or visit clients in the evening. And status in the community is no longer a differential mark of the clergy. Depending upon the community, status may be accorded for wealth or personal prestige.

Yet, the role of minister is different—perhaps not for some of the traditional reasons, but in how he is perceived. In the view of most, clergy are "holy persons." Some people view ordination as meaning the minister is closer to God and therefore privy to his special moral and spiritual guidance.

Consequently, the clergy wife is treated differently. All the attributes of ordination are projected onto her, making her special too. Ruth Truman describes how it was for her:

> Long before the first five years are up you will begin to realize that what is normal for anybody else may not be normal for you. There is a whole list of things people still frown at. Remember the first time you lost your temper and used a mild invective?

POTSHOTS AT THE PREACHER

You were as surprised as the lady who spilled her tea, but not for the same reason. You didn't expect her reaction, did you? Or how about the time they called on you to pray when you were laughing hilariously, and try as you would you never did get through the prayer? The reaction at the swim party over your bikini was a little wild. Some of those women haven't recovered yet! Things are definitely different. People *do* seem to have other expectations of you than you have of yourself.[2]

This chapter won't fit the experience of every minister's wife. Some women accept the full orbit of the clergy-wife role as their vocation and give nearly full time to it. They perceive themselves as being part of the ministry team. Many clergy spouses, however, report they feel uncomfortable with what they see as extraordinary expectations from the parish. Because they fear the criticism that may come both to themselves and their spouse, they may suppress their own feelings and comply with what others ask of them. I have identified some of the tensions that frustrate some clergy spouses and have suggested ways of resolving them.

Between a Rock and a Hard Place

Pressures from the Parish

How many times have you felt guilty, anxious, and ignorant because you preferred watching television or reading to being at another meeting? Last night you didn't feel like going to the church education committee meeting. It was one of those days that seemed more in the coping-survival column than self-fulfilling. Even as you telephoned the committee chairperson to say you wouldn't be there, you were nagged by the feeling of playing hooky. The next day a member of the committee called you to say, "We missed you at the meeting last night." Were you really missed, or are you being

CRITICISM AND THE MINISTER'S WIFE

manipulated to explain your absence? Appearing to give one message, the statement may be asking a "why" question: "Why weren't you at the meeting last night?"

"Maybe I should have gone," you think to yourself as your brain signals your guilt reflex. "I wonder what they're thinking of me."

"Why" questions disguised as statements usually carry the intention of the person making it. When you say to a child, "You didn't make your bed this morning," you are stating two intentions: (1) Give me a reason for not making your bed (the "why" question), and (2) I want you to make your bed (your real intention).

If you are sensitive to criticism, you may resent what you perceive to be pressure to give account of yourself. For example, if someone says, "I tried all morning to call you, but your phone was busy," you might resent what you interpret to be an indirect request to explain. The statement may not carry any pressure at all. What we perceive to be criticism or pressure from others may be nothing more than our own sensitivity to disapproval and mistaken assumptions about the other person. In the first example, the committee member who calls to say you were missed may mean just that, and may be expressing genuine concern. The real pressure may not be "out there" at all, but from inside you.

Pressures from Your Spouse

Have you ever felt pressured with: "Honey, can you take the junior-high church school class this morning? The teacher has called in sick, and they can't get anyone to teach it." The week has been horrendous, and you had planned to relax after breakfast. You sense your spouse's gentle, desperate urging. If you don't teach the class, he will; so you hurriedly dress,

POTSHOTS AT THE PREACHER

thinking, "But what about me? Don't I count? Must I always play the 'you can count on her' role?"

Another significant pressure on ministers' wives was identified in a 1970 study. It pointed to the heavy reliance of clergy on their spouses for positive, noncritical feedback.

> It is extremely difficult to think of any other profession in which the praise of the spouse is so intricately woven into the feeling of accomplishment as it is in the ministry. It helps us understand why many wives are so emotionally involved with the feelings of their husbands regarding their work. It also helps to underscore the feeling of isolation which is felt by clergy and causes them to rely so heavily upon their spouse for praise.[3]

Undoubtedly this creates tension at those points where you would like to offer helpful critique of a sermon or class, but you sense your husband is looking for a different message. Do you offer what he's wanting to hear, or do you speak your mind?

More difficult than any personal faultfinding is coping with criticism directed toward your spouse. When your minister-husband is being criticized, you observe how it affects him and your first impulse is to defend him. Or out of anger you may withdraw from the church in protest (refuse to take Communion) or do just the opposite (redouble your own activity in the church to make up for the weaknesses). In some instances the clergy wife has taken her spouse's criticism so personally that she has launched her own counterattack, making reconciliation virtually impossible.

Pressures from Within

When the clergy wife receives criticism, she does it without benefit of ordination, vestments, authority of office, or any of the other attributes of ministry. If you have not thought through

CRITICISM AND THE MINISTER'S WIFE

your own relationship with the church, with your husband, and with yourself, you're probably feeling internal conflicts. On the one hand, role pressure—as you learned about it from other wives, seminary days (if you were married then), and your own inner "shouldism"—dictates you should do this or that. But deep down you may want something else. Ultimately, the issue is, How willing are you to risk being yourself rather than giving in to what you think others expect of you?

In John Updike's acerbic novel, *A Month of Sundays*, a troubled Tom Marshfield says of his wife, "Being a minister's wife is curiously isolating, you're always being nice to people as a formality, you forget to feel."[4]

Being Yourself Without Feeling Guilty

When you define yourself by your role, then who you are and what you want in life will be always filtered through that role.

If being a good minister's wife means seeking and getting goodwill from everyone, it is an illusive goal. When you think you have reached it, the bells of midnight toll and the carriage turns into a pumpkin. No matter how hard you try to please, someone is sure to disagree with you, praise you, or criticize you. If you don't do enough, a few will chide you for being aloof, and if you really jump in, others will see you as trying to take over.

How do you really feel about yourself? Do you like *you?* Assertiveness psychology, a new approach to building and maintaining self-respect, says the more you stand up for yourself and act in a manner you respect, the more you will be comfortable with yourself. By exercising basic rights of being a person, you can change your attitudes and feelings about yourself. This is not an easy process since assertiveness seems to be painful for many women.

POTSHOTS AT THE PREACHER

The minister's wife is squeezed between two sets of role pressures, both circumscribed by long-standing social traditions. On one hand, you are caught between conforming to the normal sexist role definitions; yet, on the other, you have to cope with those prescribed by the role designation "Minister's Wife." Any attempt to cope with the basic problem of being female in our society will undoubtedly force a redefinition of the role of minister's wife. Learning to act assertively, *i.e.,* being your own person under all circumstances, may not always harmonize with traditional expectations of the clergy wife.

Another way of looking at this unique problem is developmentally. Five years from now you will not be the person you are today; ten years from now you will be different than when you are five years older. As you have new experiences, meet life's pressures, and undergo shifts in outlook, your needs and expectations will change. The minister's wife's role, if taken as a once-for-all-time commitment without occasional review as to what it demands from you as well as gives in return, may give rise to feelings of entrapment. The problem is to discover first what it means to be a woman in our society and then what it means to maintain your integrity amid more complex expectations.

Be Your Own Judge About Yourself

You are responsible for your own life. The Holy Spirit may give guidance, but you make decisions and accept their consequences. The wife of a minister has three options to guide her actions.

The first option is to be what others expect you to be, even if you feel differently. Meredith Wells describes how it was for her:

CRITICISM AND THE MINISTER'S WIFE

> No one worked harder or more successfully. . . . I dispatched my duties as spiritual-life chairman of the women's group . . . delivered keynote addresses for special occasions . . . cooked . . . covered dishes for the sick and . . . for the bereaved, to say nothing of covered dishes for an endless succession of covered-dish suppers. And I cleaned, of course—the church at times as well as the parsonage, and on occasion even the cemetery. I got out the bulletin . . . I directed Bible schools, organized girls' clubs, trained teachers, and conducted Sunday School contests. When not in the choir, I was heard at the piano. . . .
>
> And I was perfectly miserable.[5]

This style of life is other-directed. You consider your own feelings and wants only if no one has made prior claim on you.

The second option is at the other extreme. It urges you to repudiate all traditional roles, refrain from all usual expectations of the minister's wife, and pursue your own interests regardless of their consequences. This option is sometimes expressed by not attending worship or participating infrequently. This is a difficult option for the clergy spouse because it doesn't fit expectations, and others in the congregation may have difficulty understanding it. If expectations between you and the church about your role and level of participation in parish activities have not been clearly understood at the time of appointment or call, your pursuit of this option will inevitably lead to some problems with relationships in the church. Therefore it is important to discuss your plans thoroughly in the interviews prior to accepting a new position.

A third option finds validity somewhere between the other two. It recognizes the tensions between two significant realities—the reality of you as a person with unique interests and abilities, and the realities of your situation. On the one hand, you do not let yourself be controlled by the expectations and plans of parishioners; but, on the other, you communicate in whatever ways you deem appropriate that you appreciate them and support your husband's ministry. Beverly Davison, a Madison, Wisconsin, clergy spouse, calls this *balanced acceptance:* "The question is not what a minister's wife does, but how she does it. Willingness to do something and an enthusiasm about the church and the people can make up for a lot of missed meetings."

At times you may decide to take on a certain task because you are genuinely interested in doing it and have the ability. Or you may do it out of consideration of the needs of your husband. Still, the choice is yours.

Let Others Know You As You Are

In the preface of *The Transparent Self,* Sidney Jourard writes: "A choice that confronts every one of us at every moment is this: Shall we permit our fellow men to know us as we now are, or shall we seek instead to remain an enigma, an uncertain quantity, wishing to be seen as something we are not?"[6] It is not enough to think differently about yourself, to stay home instead of attending a meeting, or to decline to pour tea at the next social. You have to communicate to others what you think, how you feel, and what you want.

As long as you conceal your true being you keep others guessing about you. They see you, speak to you, touch you, but they don't know you as you really are. You may feel safe in your concealment—protected from criticism—but you become a nonperson.

You can learn to communicate thoughts and feelings just by doing it. Let others know where you stand by using phrases such as "I think . . ." "I feel . . ." "I want . . ." Then you and they have something to discuss. When you send clear,

CRITICISM AND THE MINISTER'S WIFE

unequivocal "I" messages, you communicate that you value yourself and that you have a right to your thoughts:

> "I appreciate your invitation, but I have made other plans."
> "I feel uncomfortable about what you're asking of me."
> "I'm really not qualified to give a talk on that."
> "Thank you, I'd like to come."

By speaking for yourself, you give people more than a role; you give them yourself.

Say No and Mean It

How comfortable are you at saying no and meaning it? Or when you say no, do you have afterthoughts about whether you did the right thing? Sharon Chace, a New Jersey minister's wife, says: "The times when I must say no are the moments when I am acutely aware of what people expect of me. . . . This insistent pressure to attend meetings . . . is just as distressing to me as conscious manipulation would be."[7] There's something inside us that prods us to say yes when we really mean no. It is easier to go to the meeting or bake cookies than to think up excuses and feel guilty. The problem is compounded because the minister's wife has more people making requests of her. Every invitation carries an enthusiastic and implied "you can't refuse" message.

There are no rule books to tell you how to say no without offending. A team of University of Wisconsin researchers, however, have developed a pencil and paper exercise to teach us how to be firm and assertive in declining invitations and requests. I have adapted their method to fit some situations likely to be encountered in the church.[8]

Step 1. Three mini-situations are given below. Read each one carefully and then write out in full how you would say no.

POTSHOTS AT THE PREACHER

Situation One:
The president of the women's association meets you after church: "Would you lead devotions and say a few words at the next meeting?" (Assuming that speaking before a group is stressful for you, how would you decline?)

Situation Two:
An elderly parishioner living alone, casually, but frequently, invites you to visit. On Saturday afternoon when you had planned to take your children to the movies, she calls and says, "I was thinking about you today; I'd like you to come over this afternoon for some fresh-baked cookies and tea." (This is the last day the movie will be shown.)

Situation Three:
A group of women have been meeting for years every third Thursday morning to sew for missions. They have seen and admired the clothes you have made for your family. One of the women, affectionately called Aunt Mary, asks you to join the group. (You really don't want to be a part of that particular group.)

Step 2. Compare your negative answers to the following instructional models. You don't have to use the same phrasing, but try to be brief, clear, and firm.

Situation One:
"Betty, I must say no to your request. I don't feel comfortable doing it."

"No, thank you, Betty. I'm willing to do other tasks, but not that one."

"No, Betty, I don't really like to speak before groups."

Situation Two:
"No, I can't come this afternoon; I promised to take the

CRITICISM AND THE MINISTER'S WIFE

children to the movie, and this is the last day it will be shown."

"No, I'm busy this afternoon, but if you'll save a cookie, I'll drop by tomorrow after church."

Situation Three:

"Aunt Mary, I can't meet with you regularly, but I'll sew with you this week."

"Aunt Mary, I appreciate being asked to join you, but I really can't."

"No, I'm sorry I can't join you. Thursday is the only day I really have to myself."

Step 3. Now it's your turn to formulate your own situations. Make them as real as you can. Use a tape recorder to practice saying no. Then listen to your voice and imagine that you're the person making the request. Is your response clear and succinct, without overly defending your actions? Practice until you're satisfied.

Step 4. When you say no in real life situations, keep your voice firm and report whatever self-awareness you think is appropriate to the situation. This is much more effective and personally satisfying than going into overly explained reasons. Then enjoy the rest of the day.

Approach Life Intentionally

Have you ever kicked a pebble into a fast-moving stream and watched what happens to it? The stone bounces along the bottom, bumps against a submerged tree stump, follows swiftly along, and then rests momentarily at the bottom of a pocket gouged out by one of the eddies. Fluctuation in the current soon jars it loose to continue its random, hapless journey toward an unknown destination. Some people approach life like the powerless pebble. They let events happen, accept the vicissitudes, and let others make their decisions for them.

Although many clergy wives are full-time housewives, a larger number are combining the homemaking role with going to school, working at a career, or volunteerism. Whatever your vocation, you can be intentional about your life; that is, think about your needs and your wants, set goals, and establish a plan to achieve them.

Nena and George O'Neill speak of creating your own challenges to deliberately test yourself in new situations.[9] This does not necessarily mean giving up homemaking to go back to school or to pursue a career. It means taking on some task larger than yourself, learning new skills, and retooling old ones. It means taking a risk and being surprised by what you can do and how well you can do it. Unlike the pebble pushed along with the force of the current, you take responsibility for the direction of your life.

To approach life intentionally requires a fair amount of psychological energy and some plain rational thought. Some night when dinner is over and you have the evening to yourself, take pencil and paper and organize your dreams around these four basic questions:

1. What do I need/want?
2. What are the resources available to me?
3. What are the limitations?
4. How can I measure progress toward goals?

A plan is only as good as the first step you take. Probably the biggest difficulty is taking that first step. This is the inertia hurdle. Several years ago the doctor wanted to check my kidney's functioning and ordered a radiological test. He sent me

CRITICISM AND THE MINISTER'S WIFE

home with a two-ounce bottle of castor oil and told me to take it that night. I knew I had to have the test, but the thought of swallowing castor oil haunted me most of the day. I also fantasized what the night would be like.

I remember pouring that foul stuff into a tablespoon, and, feeling sick and immobilized, I wanted to throw it away. I paced between the living room and kitchen. Seeing the kitchen clock, I concentrated on the second hand and vowed I would swallow the castor oil before it made a complete revolution. It worked.

It is easier to talk about what you are going to do than doing it. After you know what you want, outline the steps you have to take along the way. Jot down definite deadlines starting with what you will do tomorrow to get into your plan. These actions then become subgoals and help to make your project manageable. Sometimes its easier just to jump into the pool than to stand at the edge and think about how cold the water is.

Being a minister's wife can be emotionally fulfilling if you can strike a balance among all the expectations placed upon you by the church, your family, and your own needs and interests. You do not live in a vacuum, isolated from others who are important to you and who view you in a special way. Although it is important to listen to your own inner signals and accept your right to have them, you may occasionally take part in an activity just because your husband is the parish minister. *Let the choice be yours.*

PART TWO
Letting Criticism Work for You

Chapter 8
Can Criticism Help?

Throughout this book I have discussed how we generally experience criticism. Although ministers of congregations are the primary target for many kinds of criticism, lay persons active in congregational leadership also have to contend with it to a lesser degree. As I talk with secretaries, housewives, nurses, social workers, teachers, and others in the helping professions, I am struck by how both giving and receiving criticism is a universal problem.

Several months ago I was leading a group of rural mental-health workers in an exercise to test their tolerance for criticism. As the exercise drew to a close and we began to talk about it, a young, male social worker turned to his attractive female partner and said, "I feel I need to explain what I said to you and apologize for it."

The giving and receiving of negative messages between colleagues, spouses, friends, or members of a congregation is indeed difficult, but it can contribute to the growth of persons and relationships. How can we see ourselves as others see us if they are afraid to give us negative messages and if we are fearful that they might?

To ask the question, "Can criticism help?" we must also ask, "Whom does it help?" The critic may be helped by

CAN CRITICISM HELP?

venting angry feelings, but how does this help the person being criticized?

The helpfulness of criticism, regardless of the critic's intention, depends ultimately on how the receiver of the message perceives and uses it. If the message is perceived to be useful, is accepted, and changes are made, criticism is helpful. On the other hand, if you view the criticism as a put-down or punishment, then you may reject it or be ambivalent about it.

Consider these two questions as you learn to make criticism work for you: (1) How do you sort out valid from invalid criticism? (2) How do you stimulate constructive feedback?

Sorting Out Criticism

Sorting out criticism is not easy! When criticism comes your attitude is crucial to how you will manage the complaint, according to Gerard Egan, a trainer and observer of groups.[1] If you want to change, to grow, to be confronted and are willing to endure the unpleasant dimensions, you will actively invite confrontation as a way of engaging in a dialogic process. One such attitude is accepting criticism as an invitation to self-examination. Instead of trying to be right and justifying behavior, examine the issues in question. Does the critic have cause to be critical of you? What can you do that will resolve the dissonance between you and the other person?

Another attitude that reflects growthful response to critical confrontation is being open to how you are experienced by others. Sometimes we get comfortable with a behavior or a pattern of behaviors, only to find that others react adversely to them. Criticism is an opportunity to step back from ourselves and try to look at our actions from another's viewpoint.

Let us now look at some of the ways we bring criticism on ourselves.

POTSHOTS AT THE PREACHER

Idiosyncratic Behavior

Each of us has mannerisms, speech patterns, and habits that are uniquely ours. When any of these "individual differences" become compulsive, overbearing, or irritating to people, they may cause others to respond negatively. Affectations such as the too-frequent smile, the inappropriate use of gestures, or the ministerial voice that treats every word as if it is carved in stone can be terribly irritating.

I am embarrassed to recall a quirky behavior pattern that I developed some years ago in expressing familiarity with parishioners. Sometimes calling them by nicknames that I made up, I referred to one prominent church member—only in his presence—as "Doc." He didn't seem to object. One evening, however, his wife quietly took me aside and asked if I would call her husband by his first name instead of the slang term, which to her was offensive. I appreciated her directness.

Other examples of idiosyncratic behavior include being late for appointments, dressing inappropriately, and following work patterns that create problems for colleagues.

Mistakes and Poor Judgment

Ordination and sacred vows do not guarantee immunity from error. We make mistakes and act on poor judgment. Now and then our errors pass unnoticed, but they can come back to haunt us.

Good, concise speech was a matter of principle for a retired missionary and a language scholar in my first parish. He would devise ingenious plans to make me aware of mistakes in my sermon delivery. "Jim," the voice at the other end of the line began. "My dictionary is more than thirty years old and is probably out of date. Would you please check the pronounciation of 'Elijah' in your newer volume?"

CAN CRITICISM HELP?

I asked how he had heard me say it and then how he thought it should be pronounced. He was rarely wrong. To this day a number of scripture passages call to mind a good friend whose gentle, helpful criticism was truly appreciated.

Split-second decisions—or what sportswriters term "judgment calls"—are often made during pastoral work and are a potential source of criticism. There are no clear guidelines or instant replays. You respond to situations with words and actions that make sense to you at the moment, but that may not be understood or accepted. They may be wrong. I have made statements to people in crisis situations and, moments later, could read the disapproving response on their faces. Perhaps I did not understand the situation, the persons involved, or my own assumptions. The call may have been right, but the person wasn't ready for it. Fortunately most of our judgment calls work out. When they don't, however, we have to take the flak.

Misunderstandings and Disagreements

Criticism in the church is likely to come from misunderstandings arising from poor communication. Fuzzy communication in clarifying roles and responsibilities may lead to frustration. For example, you are invited to a special meeting of the Christian education committee that is considering a special problem in the Sunday church school. The invitation does not clearly explain your role in this meeting. If you neglect to ask, both minister and committee members may proceed as if everyone understands the ground rules. As church leader you may feel responsible for solving the problem (an assumption) while the committee members may not have any particular expectation. Such a meeting could end in dissatisfaction.

As an additional note, ask yourself: "Does this criticism

belong to me?" Perhaps it belongs to someone else. Because of their central leadership role in a congregation, ministers have a tendency to be overly responsible for everything that goes right or wrong. If someone fails to carry out an assignment, you may feel compelled to rescue them to avoid being blamed for *their* failure.

Getting Constructive Feedback

How open are you to feedback on what you do and how you're doing it? Do you eagerly soak up the positive, approving comments and anxiously hope that you won't hear disapproval? Do you wait for people to come to you with their evaluations? Do you communicate that it is O.K. to give you criticism? How is criticism handled in your church? Does it get said to the minister, but not to others?

Because they have an assigned leadership role in the congregation, clergy must not only expect feedback, but they have a right to it. How can you judge effectiveness and levels of competence if you live and work in a vacuum, isolated from the mirror of human responses? Lay persons carrying major leadership responsibilities also have a right to know how they are doing. Should they be immune to feedback just because they are volunteers and the minister is paid?

There is much interest today in clergy evaluation. The Academy of Parish Clergy has joined several denominations and consulting organizations to develop and experiment with techniques to measure the minister's effectiveness in what he or she does. Some plans are fairly simple and can be readily implemented; others are more complicated in their procedures and require extensive training in their use.

In spite of the evaluative techniques now being tested and marketed, clergy and congregations may be reluctant to try

CAN CRITICISM HELP?

them. Parish research specialist Loren Mead believes that ministers really want to improve their competence, but "seem highly allergic to the word 'evaluation.'"[2] Too many remember the "annual salary review" when they were excused from the room while the board discussed the budget for next year. Proposed raises, invariably tied to evaluation, often resulted in a recitation of the minister's deficits.

Congregations of 250 members or less may have to be convinced that formal evaluation methods are worthy of the time and effort needed to make them work. Researcher Carl Dudley feels that more than ministerial skill, the small church is interested in having a minister whom they can know as a person, whom they can love, and who will love them in return. Dudley concludes that seminaries have worked hard to prepare specialists and generalists with the skills of ministry, but "have not yet learned how to nourish spiritual lovers."[3] It is probably safe to assume that if the seminary cannot teach ministers to be spiritual lovers, there aren't evaluative instruments to measure this phenomenon either.

Formal evaluation is certainly useful when it is properly applied, accepted, and results in change. But it can be tyrannizing and manipulative if the people involved in it are not ready. I hope that presbyteries, conferences, and dioceses will resist legislating mandatory clergy evaluation and instead work lovingly and sensitively with clergy and congregations who need relationship counseling.

Evaluation is going on all the time in the congregation, but it is mostly random, unorganized, and often expressed negatively. How can you harness what is out there and learn from it? Applying a formal evaluative method is one way; using informal methods is another. A combination of both is probably closer to the ideal.

Informal feedback is the fastest, most direct means of

acquiring information. If you are a member or a chairperson of a committee, invite the group to regularly assess what they've done and how well they've done it. In the process you will learn something about your own effectiveness as a leader or member of the group. One way is to invite members to stand back from what they are doing, or have done, and make objective observations about the process. For example, a member may observe that the group is spending too much time on details in implementing a decision and point out that much time could be saved by delegating this to a subcommittee. This should be a subtle suggestion to you, if you're chairperson, to expedite meetings by delegating the more routine matters.

Another way of getting feedback is to provide a checklist to evaluate meetings as to (1) effectiveness of leadership, (2) communication of ideas, (3) communication of feelings, and (4) productivity.[4] Sharing and tabulating the results provide a useful profile. If you use the checklist technique, ask the group what they would like to see changed and what suggestions they would offer to bring about the changes.

Another technique is to ask a member of your congregation or someone from the outside to be an observer. The observer may use a checklist such as the one suggested above or evaluate according to some previously agreed upon criteria. You might invite the group to suggest criteria upon which the evaluation would be made.

Debriefing during meetings may be helpful in the following ways:

1. It gives permission for people to talk about their negative feelings.
2. It may encourage the silent participant to verbalize thoughts and feelings not expressed during the meeting.

CAN CRITICISM HELP?

3. It sensitizes the group to strengths and weaknesses of their interaction. How were disagreements handled? Was the group willing to listen to different points of view? Was there too little or to much dependence upon the chairperson or another member of the group?
4. It can encourage people who are working together toward common goals to be open, direct, and supportive of one another in giving criticism.
5. It helps a group examine how they arrive at decisions and whether the outcomes of the meeting match the purpose of the group.[5]

Utilize the organizational structure of your parish to get feedback. In some churches, this may come through the personnel committee.

Many churches have found that personnel committees are useful in providing a liaison between the congregation and the minister. These committees fulfill many purposes, among them, providing informal feedback, negotiating employment arrangements, and resolving grievances. High quality of lay leadership on these committees is necessary if they are to be sensitive to both the needs of the clergy and the congregation. The personnel committee should resist becoming merely a "gripe" transmitter—carrying complaints second- and third-hand to the minister.

In addition to consultation with the personnel committee, you may wish to get informal feedback by one or a combination of the following:

1. Ask committees with whom you work to offer feedback and report at a later meeting.
2. Build time into meetings for members' assessment of the process.

POTSHOTS AT THE PREACHER

3. Provide a suggestion box in the narthex and regularly invite suggestions.
4. Develop surveys that elicit clear and concise information needed for problem-solving and decision-making. This can be overused, however.
5. Put a notice in the bulletin requesting information.

The value of such feedback is that it is immediate; it is being processed by persons who share responsibility with you for a particular work in the congregation, and you own it.

Loren Mead does not discount the helpfulness of rating sheets and formal evaluative processes, so long as people engage one another face-to-face, think about common needs, ask about their work, and get up from the table saying, "Well, let's get started!"

Where do you get feedback? Wherever you can. And by asking people—encouraging them—to be direct with you. Neither the formal nor the informal methods are wholly adequate by themselves. Formal evaluation will help you to better organize feedback, and the informal approaches will give you more immediate access to information through a continuing process. Hopefully, people will get into the habit of giving regular feedback to you and to one another if they feel your support and acceptance.

Both minister and lay leaders have to take responsibility for helping a congregation develop an open and direct communication style that values criticism rather than being fearful of it. In the new language of marriage enrichment, it is an "I count—you count" attitude.[6] In spite of problems—even serious ones—angry feelings, mistakes, poor judgment, and idiosyncracies, we move toward growth when we value ourselves and others.

Chapter 9
Growing the Minister–Parish Relationship

The care and feeding of congregations is truly a testimony to the mystery of God's ways as well as his sense of humor. Throughout the ages, he has gathered his people into communities and has given them full responsibility for the treasures of faith. That God should choose to do this through congregations, so diverse and sometimes capricious, is a witness to his patience, love, and utter trust in humankind in spite of our inherent foibles.

Nevertheless, both clergy and congregations are caught in a dilemma between their aspirations and their fears. For the clergyperson there is the tension between being worthy of the call and feeling competent on one hand, and fearing failure and criticism on the other. For the congregation, there is tension between aspiring to live according to God's promises, meeting the suffering of others, wanting to feel the power of spiritual vitality, and the fear of losing self-direction to a leader who imposes his or her preconceived notions and values. The differentiation between the aspirations and the fears may be so compelling that clergy and congregations avoid confrontation and become critical of one another.

The purpose of this chapter is to help clergy and laity speak directly about all kinds of issues and concerns that move the

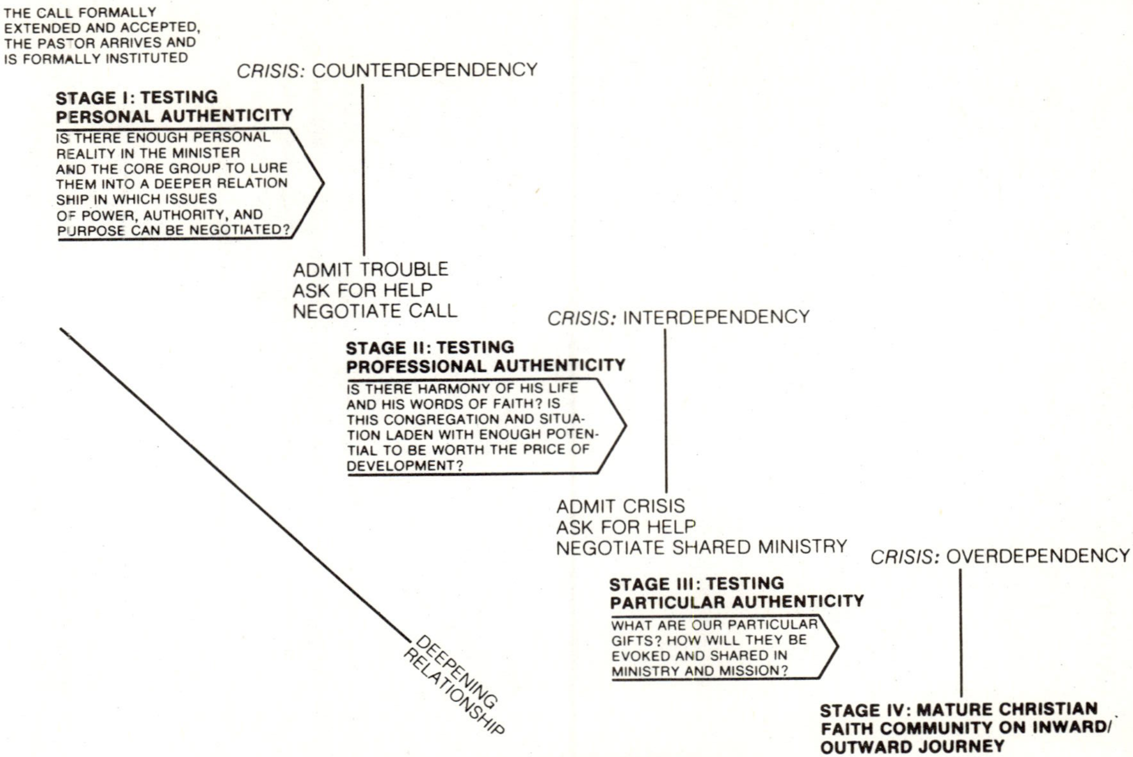
THE CALL FORMALLY EXTENDED AND ACCEPTED, THE PASTOR ARRIVES AND IS FORMALLY INSTITUTED
CRISIS: COUNTERDEPENDENCY
STAGE I: TESTING PERSONAL AUTHENTICITY
IS THERE ENOUGH PERSONAL REALITY IN THE MINISTER AND THE CORE GROUP TO LURE THEM INTO A DEEPER RELATION SHIP IN WHICH ISSUES OF POWER, AUTHORITY, AND PURPOSE CAN BE NEGOTIATED?
ADMIT TROUBLE
ASK FOR HELP
NEGOTIATE CALL
CRISIS: INTERDEPENDENCY
STAGE II: TESTING PROFESSIONAL AUTHENTICITY
IS THERE HARMONY OF HIS LIFE AND HIS WORDS OF FAITH? IS THIS CONGREGATION AND SITUATION LADEN WITH ENOUGH POTENTIAL TO BE WORTH THE PRICE OF DEVELOPMENT?
ADMIT CRISIS
ASK FOR HELP
NEGOTIATE SHARED MINISTRY
CRISIS: OVERDEPENDENCY
STAGE III: TESTING PARTICULAR AUTHENTICITY
WHAT ARE OUR PARTICULAR GIFTS? HOW WILL THEY BE EVOKED AND SHARED IN MINISTRY AND MISSION?
STAGE IV: MATURE CHRISTIAN FAITH COMMUNITY ON INWARD/ OUTWARD JOURNEY
DEEPENING RELATIONSHIP

Fig. 2. The Parish Life Process

Courtesy of the Alban Institute

GROWING THE MINISTER-PARISH RELATIONSHIP

relationship from superficiality to deeper levels of awareness and understanding. This includes discussing how leadership is carried out, arriving at common understandings of roles and responsibilities, and some plain talk about the communication process itself.

An intriguing concept of how a minister and congregation grow in their relationship has come out of Inter/Met, a congregation-based experimental seminary in Washington, D.C. Seminary president John Fletcher hypothesizes how a minister and congregation grow in their relationship. Growth is measured by three testing stages through which a congregation and its leadership must pass (see fig. 2).

After the "Honeymoon": Three Stages

Stage I: Testing Personal Authenticity

After being called to a new congregation, the minister arrives and is formally installed. The honeymoon period begins, characterized by a moritorium on not saying anything that isn't nice. Eager to demonstrate creativity, the minister may introduce some changes in the parish program. During this stage, Fletcher sees clergy and congregations "engaging in all kinds of denial and avoidance of the pain of mutual self-discovery." It is a period in which each tries to prove to the other that the call was justified. If mutual self-discovery is not pursued in this stage, however, a permanent avoidance can set in.

> The objective of the testing is to discover if there is enough personal reality in the minister and the congregation to lure them into any kind of deeper level of relationship at which the issues of power, authority, purpose, etc., can be negotiated. The role of the congregation is to test the personal reality and integrity of the

clergyperson. If they are too weak to test him or her, nothing of significance can be done with the disappointment of early hopes. The first period of mutual self-discovery is painproducing. As long as pain is avoided, growth is arrested.

It is in facing this testing period that both the minister and congregation begin to know one another and prepare to enter the next stage of relationship growth.

Stage II: Testing Professional Authenticity

Will anyone invite the minister into a serious religious relationship? Anxious about professional authority, the minister may reach beyond physical and emotional limits to prove his or her worth. Workaholism in clergy is characteristic of this stage. Because many congregational needs are presented, this is the time when the minister is easily seduced into the compassion trap, or what Fletcher calls "the madness of God."

As in the first stage, resolution depends upon how successfully the minister and the congregation work through the minister's need to be all things to all people, and the congregation's need to dump their problems on an efficient problem-solver. Fletcher asserts: "Not until the clergyperson's own experience in the congregation has the quality of living dependently on God, rather than the congregation living dependently on the leader, is the crisis transcended."

Stage III: Testing Particular Authenticity

This is the moment of truth when the minister accepts the reality that he or she can't do everything, and ministry must be shared. Interdependency, rather than dependency, characterizes this stage. Fletcher writes:

> The task of the clergyperson in this stage is to define his or her basic strengths and abilities and to focus on a possible range of

GROWING THE MINISTER-PARISH RELATIONSHIP

duties that employ those strengths. The role of the congregation is to encourage this self-definition, support a division of labor, and to assume more responsibility.

Fletcher maps the opportunities as well as the pitfalls of the minister–congregation relationship. The issue is not relationship versus no relationship. The issue is quality of relationship. Will it be full and growthful in its inclusion of pain as well as joy? Or will it be truncated and stifling in its insistence on avoiding criticism and conflict? Avoiding unpleasantness may make today easier, but in the long run the relationship suffers from its own self-denial. People may act friendly and cordial toward one another, but few take the risks that would stretch beyond what is safe and secure.[1]

In the next section I will discuss three elements that are necessary to move a relationship along in what I call "relationship talk."

Getting into Relationship Talk

Whether anxiety is caused by giving or receiving criticism, an inability to communicate accurately, or a fear of having inadequacies pointed out, the issue that clergy and congregations seem most to avoid is straight talk about their relationship. This is more than debating contractual arrangements such as salary and working conditions; it is conversation that gets inside the skin and probes those intangibles of human interaction that elude assessment in informal evaluative checklists. It is looking at such issues as trust, loyalty, and feelings. Relationship talk is being open, direct, and present to the other, reaching into the other person's world, without giving up your own, to look at your common experiences from the other's standpoint.

POTSHOTS AT THE PREACHER

Jesus regularly stepped back from his relationship with his disciples to ask, "What's going on?" Luke describes one instance:

> One time when Jesus was praying alone, the disciples came to him. "Who do the crowds say I am?" he asked them.
> "Some say that you are John the Baptist," they answered. "Others say that you are Elijah, while others say that one of the prophets of long ago has come back to life."
> (Luke 9:18-20 TEV)

But Jesus wasn't satisfied with what "people out there" thought. He wanted direct feedback from his co-workers: "What about you?" he asked. "Who do you say I am?"

Because relationships are so important for human development—they are the soil into which we were born, through which we can grow, and from which we derive our uniqueness as persons—it is imperative that we occasionally test the growing strength. Like a garden in need of regular attention, the minister–parish relationship needs shared attention by both lay and professional church leaders. If neither is willing to take the initiative, to risk the pain, to really get involved with one another, the relationship, if it exists at all, is likely to slide backwards. In counseling churches and pastors, I have seen the fallacy of the adage "No news is good news." No news may mean that the pot is boiling, yet no one is willing to talk openly and directly about it.

Consider the following ways of opening the communications channels in your congregation:

1. Confront potential relationship issues immediately.
2. Let others know you as you are.
3. Check out meanings and assumptions.

GROWING THE MINISTER-PARISH RELATIONSHIP

Confront Potential Relationship Issues Immediately

Ways we avoid pain in a relationship are (1) to walk away from a stressful issue, (2) to minimize or deny there is an issue, or (3) to postpone coping with an issue. None of these maladaptive coping methods avoids pain; they only delay it.

Recently I was asked to meet with a group of parish board members who wanted their pastor to resign. As the convenor of the meeting put it, "A number of people in the congregation want a change." Sitting informally around the kitchen table of one of the members, we spent more than two hours discussing how their minister had failed them. It was generally agreed that Jack was a competent preacher and a fine person, but he lacked administrative skills. As I probed this complaint further, one of the members who had been on the education committee said, "We were without a church school superintendent for two years, and Jack did nothing about it."

"Did you talk to him?" I asked.

"No," she replied, "he's been to seminary; he should know what to do."

Later, as other complaints were expressed about Jack's lack of initiative, I again asked, "Has anyone talked with him about this?" The closest the group came to an affirmative answer was to indicate that a brief meeting had been held two years previously to discuss some concerns that were vaguely related to their current complaints. But no one had followed up on it.

With the permission of the group, I called Jack and conveyed to him what I had learned.

"No one has come to me with any complaint," he said in surprise.

"Have you talked with any of the board members recently about your work?"

"No," he replied.

I then urged him to call a special meeting of the board to

POTSHOTS AT THE PREACHER

discuss the issue. The day after the meeting, Jack called me.

"What did you learn?" I asked.

"That I should seek another call," he said. "I know now where I stand. Believe it or not, I feel good about that!"

Unfortunately, the deterioration in Jack's relationship with his church had gone too far to mend. Each had made assumptions about the other and accepted these assumptions as the base of their relationship. As far as I could determine, many of the complaints were valid, although some did seem minor and picky. But their complaints weren't the real issue here. The issue between minister and congregation was their inability to grapple immediately with the tension-provoking issues in their relationship.

Letting Others Know You As You Are

If "depth of discovery," as Fletcher puts it, is the key to growing the pastor–parish relationship, then it is imperative that you let others know you as you are.

When you are called or appointed to a church, you step into a ready-made family where you are relatively unknown. You are an interloper, a stranger with people who have a history together, who have expectations, who have their own method of making decisions and communicating. Conflict—at the very least, criticism—may arise if you are in a healthy relationship. It will become unmanageable if you are unable or unwilling to accommodate differences between them and you.

As John Fletcher has shown, the near-fatal mistake that some clergy and congregations make is to assume that the appointment letter or certificate of call establishes *de facto* the pastor–parish relationship. These formalities are only the beginning of a process that often takes years to develop and mature. The quality of that relationship depends in part on what both minister and laity do to it—whether you will take

GROWING THE MINISTER-PARISH RELATIONSHIP

responsibility for your own expectations, fears, and wants by disclosing yourself to the other. Letting people share closeness with you helps to minimize at least two relationship barriers that plague some ministers: the clergy mystique and fear of vulnerability.

The Clergy Mystique. Reinforced by centuries of tradition, the clergy mystique is a reality that must be dealt with. It has many expressions, partly symbolized by the garb and ceremonial behavior that has frequently isolated the minister behind a wall of "holiness" and "apartness."

More than this, the clergy mystique is a bigger-than-life aura not unlike that surrounding physicians, psychiatrists, and university and seminary professors. Both the professional and the patient, client, student, or parishioner may need to keep the mystique intact to preserve a relationship held together by the illusions of the participants.

Seminary graduates usually have to face the mystique issue early in their new parish. It usually begins with tender inquiries about whether to call the new pastor "Reverend" or "pastor," or by his or her first name. One afternoon early in my first parish, in calling on an elderly woman, I said, "Please feel free to call me by my first name—Jim."

"You may call me by my last name—Mrs. Johnson!" she replied. Although she was direct, I'm glad I didn't have too many relationships like that, or I would have been very lonely.

Much more complex than whether the minister likes to be called by his or her first name or prefers a business suit to a black one, the clergy mystique hinges on how far the minister is willing to let parishioners into his or her life space and how much the parishioners want in and are willing to let the minister into theirs.

An experienced researcher in minister–congregation relationships, Loren Mead cautions young clergy against becom-

POTSHOTS AT THE PREACHER

ing too defensive or one-dimensional in their reaction to mystique issues. He believes the "mystique thing" is a way people have of saying something important about themselves:

> I think it's part of the pastor's task to be able to handle this kind of projection or dependence, be secure enough not to buy into it, and help people find the relationship they need at that time. Again, it's learning to recognize that the very presence of the pastor sets up an inner dialogue of the person with himself or herself, values, victories and defeats, as well as concept of God.[2]

The issue may not be what a person says to you or calls you, but what your presence means to that person. When mystique and role stereotypes inhibit growth in a relationship, take the risk and try to move it to a deeper level. Invite the other person to be open, direct, and self-disclosing by modeling this in your own behavior. There is the risk, though, that your openness will not be returned. So be it! You have taken a positive step forward. Anytime you go out on a limb in a relationship, you are vulnerable to possible hurt. It is still better than sitting by passively.

Your Own Vulnerability. If you hope to feel comfortable with parishioners—to meet them and be with them, to reach toward them with your weakness as well as your strength, and to trust them with *you*—then you have to take the risk of being hurt, rejected, or abandoned. When we are fearful, we feel vulnerable. And clergy seem particularly susceptible to fears such as being hurt, being wrong, and failing. Sometimes that sense of vulnerability can overpower and immobilize us.

The next time you are feeling vulnerable, ask: "What would I like to do or say in this situation? If I followed through with what I feel like saying or doing, what is the worst that could happen to me?" If somehow you can face honestly both your

GROWING THE MINISTER-PARISH RELATIONSHIP

intention—what you really want—as well as your fears about the worst that can happen, then you are well on your way to growth.

One Saturday evening a young pastor called me to discuss his anxiety about conducting a meeting of the congregation the next day; he anticipated some hostility. Deciding to take the direct approach, he said, "I'll have to screw up my guts with every ounce of strength I have, but I want to be there. I need to do it for myself." By honestly facing his worst fears beforehand, he was better able to function in the situation. He reported later that although scared, he felt better about himself.

Checking Out Meanings and Assumptions

A third element in nuturing the pastor–parish relationship is to ask of persons and groups, "What's going on with us?" If this question doesn't come from parish leaders or even from the minister (if you are a lay person), then take responsibility for asking it. This question is designed not to put others on the defensive, but (1) to get additional information, (2) to call attention to how you're communicating, and (3) to check out tentative conclusions and assumptions.

Questions of who, what, where, when, and how invite open-ended discussion. They help persons reflect and probe rather than defend or justify their actions. The process question helps maintain balance of power whereas the "why" question tends to shift power to the questioner with the other person feeling in a one-down position.

The checking-out principle is useful in coping with criticism. For example, if during a board meeting one of the members expresses concern that the youth of the church are not getting adequate clergy leadership, a checking-out procedure may help to clarify the intent of the message. Ask:

POTSHOTS AT THE PREACHER

1. Can you be specific about the problem as you understand it?
2. What are your feelings about the problem?
3. Do other members of the group have personal perceptions or feelings which will add to our understanding of the problem?
4. What suggestions have you to offer to help us/me meet this particular problem?

By asking open questions you communicate that you are genuinely interested in the problem. Avoid defensiveness by trying to understand what's going on in the situation.

One way of letting others know how you have perceived a problem is to offer them the opportunity of confirming, correcting, or rejecting your tentative conclusions. For example, when people in meetings get quiet, they are sometimes masking their anger or they have removed themselves psychologically from the group. As a participant, you have the right to ask about it. Here are some ways to check out their behavior:

"I observe that the group has gotten quiet in the past ten minutes. I'd like to ask about the meaning of the silence."

"John, you have a puzzled look on your face. Does this mean that you don't understand the proposal or that you don't agree with it?"

Checking out behavior is an important part of relationship talk. Here are some situations in which you can apply checking out skills:

1. Ask about any behavior that you think is communicating an important message, *i.e.,* unusual silences in meetings, nervous laughter, or restlessness.

GROWING THE MINISTER-PARISH RELATIONSHIP

2. Ask for reaction in those circumstances where your message or action could be misunderstood. For example, if you had to say no to an individual's request, check back later with that person to discuss any unexpressed feelings or disappointment.
3. If you are in doubt about what another person thinks or expects of you, ask!

Obviously, Fletcher's theory will not fit all clergy and parishes, just as theories of the grief process do not universally describe every person who experiences loss. And it is possible that some relationships will not tolerate depth of openness and self-disclosure because of how the participants are psychologically put together. Then, there are those not-too-rare situations in which one person is ready to be close, but the other isn't.

How you as a minister or lay person get into relationship talk—whether you come on like gang-busters or ease carefully and sensitively into it—depends on how comfortable you are with yourself and how sensitive you are to the other. It can be scary when two or more persons begin to get close to one another.

Relationship talk, if it is caring, direct, and probing, will provide a way of coping with criticism. When a minister and a board, for example, share feelings, check out assumptions, and communicate in other ways that demonstrate mutual trust and loyalty, negative messages can be expressed without the usual fear that goes with such statements as, "I wonder what was meant by that?" Instead of worrying, unnecessarily about it, ask!

Chapter 10
Closing the Perfection Gap

As an apostle, Paul had no illusions about himself:

> Yet we who have this spiritual treasure are like common clay pots, to show that the supreme power belongs to God, not to us. We are often troubled, but not crushed; sometimes in doubt, but never in despair; there are many enemies, but we are never without a friend; and though badly hurt at times, we are not destroyed. (II Corinthians 4:7-9 TEV)

Jesus and the apostles were more accepting of human vulnerability and volatility than many of us who are part of the Christian community today. And we have had several thousand years' experience to instruct us in the magnitude of earthling foibles.

Even in this enlightened age there's still a "perfection gap," at least in the minds of some, between clergy and laity. Ask the average lay person (whatever "average" means) if he or she expects clerical impeccability. Denial might be followed with a mild qualification: "Of course we don't expect our minister to be perfect, but after all, ordination should mean something." The difference between "I don't expect . . ." and "after all . . ." is the perfection gap.

The perfection gap may be the most important single barrier to real communication among clergy and lay persons. I

CLOSING THE PERFECTION GAP

experience it even now, although I no longer work as a leader of a parish. It was reported to me that a neighbor in the community where I live expressed guilt about drinking beer in her backyard because she worried about "what Jim would think." It is difficult for people to be close when this kind of gap exists. Sensing varying dimensions of this gap among lay persons, the minister may hesitate to risk criticism by letting people get close. And some people, feeling dependent and in need of a strong behavior model may not want to get too close to their minister. Both are tyrannized not only by their expectations of one another, but by their fear of disapproval and disappointment.

The perfection gap is most visible during the process of calling a new minister. There seems to be an assumption that laity are plagued with problems, suffer from spiritual dryness, and are morally naïve, while out there, somewhere, is a leader who has it together and is "just right for us." According to one national survey, such a minister is self-effacing, morally exemplar, impervious to stress, an effective communicator, a community leader, a problem-solver, a conflict negotiator, a competent theologian, and happily married or reasonably "adjusted" to celibate life.

Ministers hoping to change parishes in a tight job market may try to meet perfectionist expectations by agreeing to more than they can deliver. They may acquiesce to some expectations that are realistic but do not reflect accurately their personal priorities, interests, or competencies. The surplus of clergy and the competition for the positions that are available may prevent the depth of mutual probing that is necessary to close the perfection gap.

Frank Williams, director of the Midwest Career Development Center, differentiates among three kinds of expectations which involve—

POTSHOTS AT THE PREACHER

1. our own expectations of ourselves (both realistic and unrealistic);
2. others expectations of us (both realistic and unrealistic);
3. our projections of expectations that we believe others have of us.[1]

Grandiose and unattainable, many of these expectations elude reality. A minister, for example, wants to preach sermons in the style of yesterday's pulpit orators like Harry Emerson Fosdick, but has only limited time for sermon preparation. Consequently, the preaching is adequate, but not exceptional. On the other hand, the congregation may have an unrealistic view of what it wants the minister to do, like making thirty house calls per week.

Expectations can be realistic, but held only by one side, leading quickly to criticism and conflict if the differences are not resolved. To illustrate, a minister may expect church members to increase their giving by 20 percent next year, a clergy expectation not widely shared by the congregation. Or the congregation wants the minister to join a country club, an expectation not shared by the minister.

Recently, an "enterprising" church board lumped their expectations into a lengthy bill of particulars that they presented to the minister. There were nearly twenty items stipulating what they wanted. Heading the list was "change the bulletin board by Tuesday," and "announce the name of the flower chairman." In a bedroom community not twenty minutes from a city of two hundred thousand, the final item mandated: "Call on all newcomers to town and invite them to church." If these expectations were not carried out, the last paragraph hinted there would be a salary adjustment downward.

As this case illustrates, expectations can harden into demands that rarely can be negotiated or even discussed. The

CLOSING THE PERFECTION GAP

only option is to comply or be punished. Hopefully this young pastor will learn the skills to assertively grapple with attitudes and behaviors that are boldly dehumanizing.

Perfectionist expectations will continue to haunt the minister-congregation relationship unless one, the other, or both agree to close the gap. Any one or all three of the following procedures may be necessary, depending on the breadth of the perfection gap.

Explore Thoroughly One Another's Expectations

In his review of research highlighting the gap in clergy–lay expectations and the felt frustration, Donald Smith concludes:

1. Clergy and laity frequently have differing understandings of what the minister ought to do.
2. Clergy perceptions of the expectations of their lay leaders have been shown to be inadequate in many cases. There is a great need for dialogue so that laity and ministers can understand one another.
3. Discussion of clergy roles has proved to be an effective method of bringing lay leaders and ministers closer together. It is important to make role conflicts visible so they can be dealt with.
4. In the face of role conflict or ambiguity, people tend to withdraw rather than increase their efforts to communicate. This only makes matters worse.
5. An active stand on the part of clergy, rather than passivity, is needed if role conflict is to be reduced. This may be difficult for those ministers who are inclined toward passivity.
6. There is an urgent need for dialogue on the goal and purpose of the church's existence. Some of the confusion and disagreements that exist cut deeply into the effectiveness of the church. Lay leaders and clergy alike owe it to their people to discover where the church should be going. The complexities of the present age do not make this easy, but it must be done.[2]

POTSHOTS AT THE PREACHER

Negotiate Differences

Some conflicting expectations cannot be resolved without much discussion and possibly compromise. When people know what others expect of them, when they themselves agree to those expectations, there is more likely to be good feeling and high productivity. According to Paul Diettrich of the Center for Parish Development, negotiation is a give-and-take process. It involves two or more parties making demands, offering proposals and counter-proposals about goals of the church, the size of the budget, budget allocations, and the minister's salary.[3]

Diettrich, in teaching negotiating skills to church leaders, believes that this kind of "democracy at work" builds acceptance and trust among persons by reinforcing self-worth. Bargaining can be successful only if the parties respect and value one another throughout the process.

Besides reinforcing the other's sense of self-worth, bargaining also includes (1) identifying and testing assumptions, (2) clarifying goals, (3) identifying and building on areas of overlapping objectives, (4) holding to a meeting agenda, and (5) examining alternative solutions. Emotions may be intense, therefore time for expression of feelings and "cooling off" needs to be included.

Use Consultants to Resolve Impasses

What do you do when you reach an impasse in which each party declines to compromise further? One option is to garner your forces and precipitate a fight that may be healthy or destructive.[4] Congregations tend to be ill-equipped to fight successfully, as legions of clergy and lay leaders can attest. Another option is to confront the impasse, admit that you need

CLOSING THE PERFECTION GAP

help, and get assistance in resolving the issues. Possible resources may include (1) paid consultants from nearby universities, colleges, or seminaries, (2) people from other churches, (3) denominational staff, and (4) ecumenical agency personnel such as those associated with the Association of Clinical Pastoral Educators or the Association for Religion and Applied Behavioral Science.

Speed Leas and Paul Kittlaus urge caution in selecting a consultant to work in crisis situations. They emphasize that the person must have experience in working with groups in conflict. Select a person who has enough self-awareness to be comfortable with his or her own strengths and weaknesses. Be clear as to what you are asking that person to do. If this person is to be a mediator, then the role is to help the disputing parties identify new options that will hopefully lead to agreement. If the role is to arbitrate, then the entire burden of decision is upon the person you have called in. In essence, this is the role of judge. The decision is binding upon all parties.

Chapter 11
When You Feel Critical

Criticism, as one form of interpersonal confrontation, has many dimensions. It can be irrational and manipulative, or it can be objectively conceived and sensitively communicated—an act of deeply caring for and valuing another. There is mounting evidence that critical confrontation, even when it is blaming and punishing, can express involvement and caring. "I do not think that deep, human acceptance of others necessarily implies or is synonymous with approval," writes Gerard Egan. "If I am sincerely interested in human growth, then I do not expect my friends to accept me in the sense that they overlook, discount, or even approve of modes of acting that are antithetical to their values or that I myself am dissatisfied with."[1]

Because criticism is invariably painful and frequently laced with emotional intensity, we may avoid confronting others with criticism because we want to protect them from pain (or ourselves, out of fear they might fight back). To do so is to deny them the opportunity for growthful reflection. Needing to be "the nice guy" and to maintain relationships whatever the cost, we may avoid meaningful and appropriate confrontation.

The next time you feel critical and before you storm into the next office or room to "get it off your chest," ask yourself one or more of these questions:

WHEN YOU FEEL CRITICAL

Who Am I Criticizing? Am I talking with the right person, or am I directing negatives to a convenient and safe target? Spouses frequently take a lot of flack that has been misdirected. The same is true of a parent whom we can no longer reach directly. Communicate that you value the person toward whom you feel critical by letting your anger (if that's part of your message) be in proportion to the needs, sensitivities, and capabilities of the person you are confronting.

Why Do I Feel Critical? Do I really want to be helpful to the person? Am I angry about something else, but find criticism an easy way to vent it? Get in touch with your own immediate life-space. Are you feeling rushed and under pressure? How did you feel when you awakened this morning—eager to take on the day or BLAH?

What Am I Criticizing? If you're really angry, you may blast away at anything and everything, including past history, dredging up hurts from another day. Be specific about criticism. Identify your complaint and specify what changes you desire. The other person has a right to respond. It is possible that your criticism is based on your own misunderstanding rather than the other person's error.

Is This the Best Time and Place? It is embarrassing to be criticized before an audience, even an audience of one. If you have a negative message to give, choose a place that's private and a time that's convenient. This communicates to the other person that you have something important to communicate, and you're not trying to force your own schedule upon him or her. If your purpose is to be helpful with your negative message, anything you can do to enhance communication will be helpful.

How Can I Communicate My Criticism Effectively? "Effectively" is different from "painlessly." You may be very effective at giving a critical message, yet it is still painful to the person receiving it. Taking an "I Count—You Count" posture in delivering criticism doesn't mean protecting the other person. You cannot take responsibility for how the person will feel; you can communicate, however, that you value and respect him or her while giving the criticism. These statements might serve as useful models:

"I've been thinking about something that I'd like to talk over with you."

"John, I've been bothered by something you've been telling others about me."

"I don't know how others feel about what you said in the meeting last night, but I can report how it affected me."

In giving criticism, speak only for yourself. And don't get trapped into being the "spokesman" for people who want to remain anonymous by letting you speak for them. To imply that an unidentified army of "theys" are out there pointing fingers and criticizing is sure to instill fear in the person you're trying to help. It is unfair to use this tactic as it creates unnecessary anxiety and communicates the one-sided message: "We've chosen up sides, and you've lost."

It is a hard truth, but criticism and conflict in the church is here to stay. The issue for ministers and lay persons is not how to suppress it or avoid it, but how to get comfortable with it, use it, and help others to use it. No matter how much you may understand the sociology of groups and the dynamics of human behavior or how much you're in tune with your own inner person, criticism will come and it will hurt. Nevertheless, the same sensitivity that lets you feel the hurt may lead you to greater understanding of your own needs as well as those of others.

NOTES

CHAPTER TWO

1. Karen Horney, *The Neurotic Personality of Our Time* (New York: W. W. Norton & Co., 1937), p. 243.

2. Everett L. Shostrom, *Man, the Manipulator: The Inner Journey from Manipulation to Actualization* (New York: Bantam Books, 1967), p. 126.

3. Frank Goble, *The Third Force* (New York: Pocket Books, 1974), pp. 37-53.

4. Donald P. Smith, *Clergy in the Crossfire* (Philadelphia: The Westminster Press, 1973), pp. 60-68.

5. Sidney Jourard, *The Transparent Self: Self-Disclosure and Well-Being* (New York: Van Nostrand Reinhold Co., 1971), p. 41.

6. Allen Wheelis, *How People Change* (New York: Harper & Row, 1974), p. 73.

CHAPTER THREE

1. Nena O'Neill and George O'Neill, *Shifting Gears: Finding Security in a Changing World* (New York: Avon Books, 1974), pp. 49-63.

2. Wayne Oates, *Confessions of a Workaholic* (Nashville: Abingdon, 1971).

CHAPTER FOUR

1. George R. Bach and Herb Goldberg, *Creative Aggression* (New York: Avon Books, 1974), p. 51.

2. Clark Moustakas, *Personal Growth: The Struggle for Identity and Human Values* (Cambridge: H. A. Doyle, 1969), p. 64.

3. Gregory Rochlin, *Griefs and Discontents: The Forces of Change* (Boston: Little, Brown, 1965), p. 1.

4. Henri J. M. Nouwen, *Genessee Diary: Report from a Trappist Monastery* (Garden City, N.Y.: Doubleday & Co., 1976), p. 57.

POTSHOTS AT THE PREACHER

5. Leo Madow, *Anger* (New York: Charles Scribner's Sons, 1972), pp. 1-90.

6. Fritz Perls, *The Gestalt Approach and Eyewitness to Therapy* (Ben Lomond, Calif.: Science & Behavior Books, 1973), p. 64.

7. Leonard Berkowitz, "The Case for Bottling Up Rage" *Psychology Today,* 7 (July, 1973), 24-30.

8. Edgar Jackson, *Coping with the Crises in Your Life* (New York: Hawthorn Books, 1974), p. 133.

9. The Society of Continuing Education for Ministry, 855 Locust Street, Collegeville, Pennsylvania, has listings of continuing education programs and other literature to help you plan your own program.

10. Mark Rouch, *Competent Ministry: A Guide to Effective Continuing Education* (Nashville: Abingdon, 1974).

11. Thomas Kelly, *A Testament of Devotion* (New York: Harper & Brothers, 1941), pp. 29-31.

12. Jess Lair, *I Ain't Much, Baby—But I'm All I've Got* (New York: Doubleday & Co., 1972), p. 55.

CHAPTER FIVE

1. Stanley Lesse, ed., *Masked Depression* (New York: Jason Aronson, 1974), p. 78.

2. Bach and Goldberg, *Creative Aggression,* p. 69.

3. *Ibid.,* p. 76.

4. Else Frenkel-Brunswik, "Adjustments and Reorientation in the Course of the Life Span," in *Middle Age and Aging: A Reader on Social Psychology,* ed. Bernice L. Neugarten (Chicago: University of Chicago Press, 1968), p. 7.

5. Raymond G. Kuhlen, "Developmental Changes in Motivation During the Adult Years," *ibid.,* pp. 115-36.

6. T. H. Holmes and R. H. Rahe, "The Social Readjustment Rating Scale," *Journal of Psychosomatic Research,* 11(1967), 213-18.

7. Donald Goergen, *The Sexual Celibate* (New York: The Seabury Press, 1974), p. 156.

8. Adapted from J. W. Getzels and E. G. Guba, "Social Behavior and the Administrative Process," *School Review,* 65 (Winter, 1957), 423-41.

CHAPTER SIX

1. Eric Berne, *Games People Play* (New York: Grove Press, 1964), pp. 85-88.

2. Stanlee Phelps and Nancy Austin, *The Assertive Woman* (Fredericksburg: Impact, 1975), pp. 34-46.

NOTES TO PAGES 42-94

3. Sherod Miller, Elam W. Nunnally, Daniel B. Wackman, *Alive and Aware* (Minneapolis: Interpersonal Communications Programs, 1975), p. 165.

4. Howard J. Clinebell, Jr., with Harvey Siefert, *Personal Growth and Social Change* (Philadelphia: The Westminster Press, 1969), pp. 186-90.

CHAPTER SEVEN

1. Problems confronting clergy wives may be different from those facing the husbands of women ministers. Some of the issues that I address here have evolved from a long-standing tradition of sex and role stereotyping. At present there is little or no literature available on the male clergy spouse.

2. Ruth Truman, *Underground Manual for Ministers' Wives* (Nashville: Abingdon, 1974), p. 12.

3. Frank C. Williams, "Some Perspectives on the Needs of Clergy—Personal and Professional," mimeographed (Columbus, Ohio: Midwest Career Development Center, 1970).

4. John Updike, *A Month of Sundays* (New York: Fawcett Crest Books, 1975), p. 78.

5. Meredith Wells, "Thrice I Cried, Or, How to Be a Minister's Wife If You Loathe It," *Talk 'n' Thought* (September, 1975), p. 6. This is a new journal published quarterly by clergy wives for clergy wives. Well written and attractively presented, it strikes a balance between role problems and satisfactions. Write to *Talk 'n' Thought,* 901 West 24th Street, Austin, Texas 78705.

6. Jourard, *Transparent Self,* p. iii.

7. Sharon R. Chace, "The Minister's Wife," *The Christian Ministry,* January, 1976, pp. 1515.

8. Richard M. McFall and Craig T. Twentyman, "Four Experiments on the Relative Contributions of Rehearsal Modeling and Coaching to Assertion Training," *Journal of Abnormal Psychology,* 81 (June, 1973).

9. O'Neill and O'Neill, *Shifting Gears,* pp. 1-40.

CHAPTER EIGHT

1. Gerard Egan, *Face to Face: The Small-Group Experience and Interpersonal Growth* (Monterey: Brooks/Cole Publishing Co., 1973), pp. 129-31.

2. Loren Mead, "Clergy Evaluation: Who Owns It?" (Washington, D.C.: Alban Institute, 1974), p. 2.

3. Carl Dudley, "Unique Dynamics of the Small Church" (McCormick Seminary, March, 1976), p. 10.

4. Philip A. Anderson, *Church Meetings That Matter* (Philadelphia: United Church Press, 1965), p. 49.

POTSHOTS AT THE PREACHER

5. For a fuller discussion see Gerold Apps, *Ideas for Better Church Meetings* (Minneapolis: Augsburg Publishing House, 1975), p. 120.

6. George Calden, *I Count—You Count* (Niles, Ill.: Argus Communications, 1976).

CHAPTER NINE

1. John Fletcher, "Religious Authenticity in the Clergy: Implications for Theological Education" (Washington, D.C.: Alban Institute, 1975).

2. Mead, in correspondence with the author.

CHAPTER TEN

1. Frank Williams, "What's Going On in the Clergy Profession" (Workshop conducted at the University of Wisconsin, September 20, 1975).

2. Smith, *Clergy in the Crossfire*, p. 142.

3. Paul Diettrich and Charles Ellzey, "The Pastor As Bargainer," *The Center Newsletter*, 5 (April, 1975).

4. For a fuller discussion of conflict in the church, see Speed Leas and Paul Kittlaus, *Church Fights: Managing Conflict in the Local Church* (Philadelphia: The Westminster Press, 1973).

CHAPTER ELEVEN

1. Egan, *Face to Face*, p. 94.

Resources

The following list is representative of groups who are currently engaged in trying to improve the art of ministry within the local parish.

Academy of Parish Clergy, Inc., 409 Greenfield, Oak Park, Illinois 60302. Members receive the *Guide for Continuing Growth,* a well-conceived plan for clergy self-evaluation using outside feedback. Publishes a journal and other continuing-education resources.

Alban Institute, Mt. St. Alban, Washington, D.C. 20016; Loren Mead, director. This agency is studying how the parish system can be made more healthy. Staff and associates have expertise in training interim pastors and vacancy consultation. List of monographs is available upon request.

Association for Creative Change, P. O. Box 437, Wilmette, Illinois 60091. A professional association for trainers and consultants. Contact them for names of persons and agencies doing skill training in conflict management.

Berkeley Center for Human Interaction, 1816 Scenic Avenue, Berkeley, California 94709; Trevor Hoy, director. A training and consulting agency for clergy and congregations, making good use of nearby seminaries and universities.

Center for Parish Development, 320 East School Avenue, Naperville, Illinois 60540; Paul Diettrich, director. A research and parish-renewal center that is related to The United Methodist Church, but is ecumenical in its work. Publishes an excellent newsletter.

Church Career Development Council, 475 Riverside Drive, Room 770, New York, New York 10027. Write for a list of fourteen centers across the country specializing in clergy career assessment.

Enablement Information Service, Inc., 8 Newbury Street, 4th Floor, Boston, Massachusetts 02116; James Lowery, Jr., director. A one-of-its-kind agency involving five hundred persons in a national information network on clergy development. Subscription to newsletter and occasional papers is ten dollars annually.

Judicatory Career Support System, 3501 Campbell, Kansas City, Missouri 64109; Eugene E. Timmons, director. Is developing a clergy-assessment program that spans most of the year with monthly focus on particular aspects of ministry. Combines self-assessment with peer and congregation feedback within a support group context.

Lyle E. Schaller, 530 N. Brainard Street, Naperville, Illinois 60540. Lyle Schaller serves as a parish consultant for the *Yokefellow Institute,* Richmond, Indiana. He spends approximately one hundred days each year in consultation with congregations and clusters of churches, and another one hundred days as a resource person for workshops on parish planning, cooperative ministries, Christian education, church growth, planned change, futurism, and multiple-staff ministries.

Society for the Advancement of Continuing Education for Clergy (SACEM), 855 Locust Street, Collegeville, Pennsylvania 19426; Connolly Gamble, executive secretary. Professional society for all persons interested in continuing education for ministry. Publishes annual regional listings of

RESOURCES

programs. Has published a survey of procedures being used by clergy in personal and professional assessment for planning their own continuing education.

Toward the Improvement of Ministry. A series of instruments to aid pastors and congregations in setting goals and evaluating effectiveness in achieving them. Developed jointly by the Vocation Agency of the United Presbyterian Church in the U.S.A., 475 Riverside Drive, Room 420, New York, New York 10027, and the General Executive Board of the Presbyterian Church in the U.S., 341 Ponce de Leon Avenue, N.E., Atlanta, Georgia 30308.

Bibliography

Anderson, Philip A. *Church Meetings That Matter.* Philadelphia: United Church Press, 1965.

Apps, Gerold. *Ideas for Better Church Meetings.* Minneapolis: Augsburg Publishing House, 1975.

Bach, George R., and Goldberg, Herb. *Creative Aggression.* New York: Avon Books, 1974.

Berkowitz, Leonard. "The Case for Bottling Up Rage." *Psychology Today,* July, 1973, pp. 24-30.

Berne, Eric. *Games People Play.* New York: Grove Press, 1964.

Calden, George. *I Count—You Count.* Niles, Ill.: Argus Communications, 1976.

Chase, Sharon R. "The Minister's Wife." *The Christian Century,* January, 1976, p. 1515.

Clinebell, Howard Jr., with Siefert, Harvey. *Personal Growth and Social Change.* Philadelphia: The Westminster Press, 1969.

Dietterich, Paul, and Ellzey, Charles. "The Pastor As Bargainer." *The Center Letter* 5 (April, 1975).

Fletcher, John, "Religious Authenticity in the Clergy: Implications for Theological Education," Monograph. Washington, D.C.: Alban Institute, 1975.

Getzels, J. W., and Guba, E. G., "Social Behavior and the Administrative Process." *School Review* 65 (Winter, 1957), pp. 423-41.

Goble, Frank. *The Third Force.* New York: Pocket Books, 1974.

Goergen, Donald. *The Sexual Celibate.* New York: The Seabury Press, 1974.

Harris, John. "The Minister Looks for a Job," Monograph. Washington D.C.: Alban Institute, 1974.

Holmes, T. H., and Rahe, R. H., "The Social Readjustment Rating Scale." *Journal of Psychosomatic Research* 11 (1967), 213-18.

BIBLIOGRAPHY

Horney, Karen. *The Neurotic Personality of Our Time*. New York: W. W. Norton & Co., 1937.

Howe, Reuel L. *The Miracle of Dialogue*. New York: The Seabury Press, 1963.

Jackson, Edgar N. *Coping with the Crises in Your Life*. New York: Hawthorn Books, 1974.

Jourard, Sidney M. *The Transparent Self: Self-Disclosure and Well-Being*. New York: Van Nostrand Reinhold Co., 1971.

Kelly, Thomas. *A Testament of Devotion*. New York: Harper & Brothers, 1941.

Lair, Jess. *I Ain't Much, Baby—But I'm All I've Got*. New York: Doubleday & Co., 1972.

Leas, Speed, and Kittlaus, Paul. *Church Fights: Managing Conflict in the Local Church*. Philadelphia: The Westminster Press, 1973.

Lesse, Stanley, ed. *Masked Depression*. New York: Jason Aronson, 1974.

Madow, Leo. *Anger*. New York: Charles Scribner's Sons, 1972.

McFall, Richard M., and Twentyman, Craig T. "Four Experiments on the Relative Contributions of Rehearsal Modeling and Coaching to Assertiveness Training." *Journal of Abnormal Psychology*, June, 1973.

Mead, Loren. "Clergy Evaluation: Who Owns It?" Monograph. Washington, D.C.: Alban Institute, 1974.

Miller, Sherod; Nunnally, Elam W.; and Wackman, Daniel B. *Alive and Aware*. Minneapolis: Interpersonal Communication Programs, Inc., 1975.

Moustakas, Clark. *Personal Growth: The Struggle for Identity and Human Values*. Cambridge: H. A. Doyle, 1969.

Neugarten, Bernice L., ed. *Middle Age and Aging: A Reader on Social Psychology*. Chicago: University of Chicago Press, 1968.

Nouwen, Henri J. M. *Genessee Diary: Report from a Trappist Monastery*. Garden City, N.Y.: Doubleday & Co., 1976.

Oates, Wayne. *Confessions of a Workaholic*. Nashville: Abingdon, 1971.

O'Neill, Nena, and O'Neill, George. *Shifting Gears: Finding Security in a Changing World*. New York: Avon Books, 1974.

Perls, Fritz. *The Gestalt Approach and Eyewitness to Therapy*. Ben Lomond, Calif.: Science & Behavior Books, 1973.

Phelps, Stanlee, and Austin, Nancy. *The Assertive Woman*. Fredericksburg: Impact, 1975.

POTSHOTS AT THE PREACHER

Rochlin, Gregory. *Griefs and Discontents: The Forces of Change.* Boston: Little, Brown, 1965.

Rouch, Mark. *Competent Ministry: A Guide to Effective Continuing Education.* Nashville: Abingdon, 1974.

Smith, Donald. *Clergy in the Crossfire.* Philadelphia: The Westminster Press, 1973.

Truman, Ruth. *Underground Manual for Ministers' Wives.* Nashville: Abingdon, 1974.

Updike, John. *A Month of Sundays.* New York: Fawcett Crest Books, 1975.

Wells, Meredith, "Thrice I Cried, Or, How to Be a Minister's Wife If You Loathe It." *Talk 'n' Thought,* September, 1975, p. 6.

Wheelis, Allen. *How People Change.* New York: Harper & Row, 1970.

Williams, Frank C. "Some Perspectives on the Needs of Clergy—Personal and Professional." Mimeographed. Columbus, Ohio: Midwest Career Development Center, 1970.